TRIED
TO BE STRAIGHT
OPTIONS FOR GAY CHRISTIANS

ANDY WELLS

For more information, or information regarding subsidiary rights, please contact the author at andy@triedtobestraight.com

Edited by: Megan Hershenson

Cover Design and Formatting by: Rebecca Manuel, Bibliophile Productions

Printed in the United States of America

First Printing, August 2021

ISBN: 978-1-946061-92-8

CONTENTS

FOREWORD

Congratulations on giving yourself the gift of reading this book! *Tried to be Straight,* by my friend and writing colleague Andy Wells, is the perfect present for Christians who are not straight – and are looking for indispensable tools to help them thrive at the intersection of their love for Jesus and their authentic sexuality.

Many authors write formulas for how to succeed, wherein they convince you to think and act as the author does in order to have a happy life. Andy's book is refreshingly different: he provides you the vital tools to partner with the Holy Spirit in figuring out your best self. And since Jesus already accepts you exactly as you are, you are going to really benefit from reading this book!

You, the gay Christian, have already been given plenty of guidance – and demands! – on how you should think, identify, and behave. Andy Wells oozes a heart of compassion – longing to come alongside you in your confusion and pain rather than scowl above you. It is typically very daunting and draining to make sense of your gayness – as Andy and I well know.

Both of us left our original family's faith and became born-again followers of Jesus. And, in both of our cases, our conversion was real and lasting. Then, we went on to become evangelicals – where we developed a love and reverence for the Bible as a source of God's truth. We both were deeply influenced by evangelical denominations, pastors, ministries, and friends. And we both were keenly aware of our attraction to men, gave our best efforts to change our sexual orientation, and could not change.

Furthermore, we both stayed closeted until mid-life. In Andy's closeted situation, he excelled in the evangelical community - earning a master's degree in apologetics from an esteemed evangelical university. In my closeted case, I became vice president of America's most influential evangelical ministry from 1995-2004: Focus on the Family. Later, Andy would develop a certainty of God's love for him as a gay man and embrace an affirming theology and relationships. Likewise, I became convinced of Jesus' love for me – exactly as I am. Subsequently, I had a successful career as a licensed professional counselor, coach, and mentor in assisting thousands of gay Christian men in overcoming shame rather than attempting sexual orientation change.

And gosh, I would have loved to have had this book much earlier in my journey!

Andy's gentle, reasonable posture does not demand the reader change his current position (whether traditional or progressive, embracing celibacy or affirming gay marriages). The majority of this book looks at perspectives of conservative evangelicals, plus an additional lens. The chapters focus on the bedrock issues facing every gay Christian: attraction, lust, sexual behavior, marriage, coming out, and selecting the best fitting church for your giftings. And, as you will soon discover, the book does not use a "lawyer" approach of only providing evidence that will force you (as the reader) to come to one and only one viable conclusion. Nor does this book demand revolution – out with the old, in with the new! Instead, with tender care and scholarly citations, the author allows you to place one idea in your right palm, a different idea in your left, and invites you to fearlessly look at both simultaneously – with malice toward none and justice for all.

I found several of Andy's chapters to be masterful and unique (which is saying a lot because I thought I had already read all that is of value regarding being gay and Christian). And I appreciated the book's conciseness. Trust me, you (the reader) would need to consume three to five other excellent books to attain this book's chock-full information. *Tried to be Straight* is so expertly and lovingly written that I often found myself cheering, "Bravo, Andy!" The book allows you to grab a warm mug of coffee, cuddle next to the Holy Spirit, and safely come up with your conclusions. And my hunch is that God wants you to be at your authentic best in providing Jesus' selfless love to all others.

That is enough from me - I want you to begin reading the excellent stuff! As for me, I will be recommending – no, buying! – this book for all of my gay Christian friends who seek me out for counsel and encouragement. Thanks, Andy, for this landmark contribution to a Christian culture currently stuck in antagonistic positions. Bravo, indeed!

Dr. Mike Rosebush

Former Vice President - Focus on the Family

Lover of Jesus; Ph.D. in Counseling Psychology; author of books on assisting gay Christians; retired licensed professional counselor, coach, and mentor to thousands of gay Christians. Currently, a friend to all. He may be reached at mikerosebush75@gmail.com and https://www.facebook.com/mike.rosebush.7/

PREFACE

In the middle of San Francisco's financial district, my friend Don hosted his bi-annual Holiday Music Jam and Singalong, where everyone was encouraged to bring their song requests to sing and play along with the half-dozen professional musicians in attendance. The eighth floor, one-bedroom apartment overflowed with food, people, and music. With my mom in the hospital, my employer on the brink of bankruptcy, and the holiday stresses that come with every December, I welcomed the opportunity to relax, smile, and sing.

One of the things that always made this event special was the mix of people. They were of different religions (Christian, Jewish, Muslim, Pagan), married people, polyamorous throuples, straight people, gay people, trans people, sober folks, drinkers, and the list went on. The group enjoyed singing together – making such a din that dog walkers in the park eight stories below would stop and stare to see where all the noise was coming from.

The only rule at Don's holiday music jam was…no holiday

music. Don hosted a summer music jam in July where Christmas songs were allowed. Not so in December!

The mere suggestion of holiday music brought about eye rolls and scowls – a knee-jerk fear of continuing what we listened to in grocery stores and coffee houses 24/7. Seeing an opportunity for humor, I grabbed the sleigh bells out of the basket of percussion instruments provided for us lay-musicians and inserted their Christmassy cheer into the music of the Beatles, Alicia Keys, and Elton John. It threw everyone off at first, but they quickly realized sleigh bells were not on the list of prohibited items and laughed along with me.

When the joke got a little stale, I headed to the balcony to enjoy the cool, moist bay air and the stellar evening lights of the East Bay, Bay Bridge, and Coit Tower. That's where I met Ann.

Ann looked to be in her late thirties. She wore a long, patterned dress that fell somewhere between casual and "nice party." Her long brown hair and glasses completed a look that made me feel at ease with her immediately. So often in San Francisco I was surrounded by people with a political axe to grind, but this was not so with Ann. Our conversation turned to church and religion, as it often does with me. Ann was really interested in my church, which I described as "whacky."

Ann responded by sharing her son's story with me. She described to me what it was like to watch Darrell come out at age 13. How he enjoyed church, loved Jesus, and was searching for options to live in a way that honored both. Their church was a conservative, evangelical brand that split from its denomination over the acceptance of gay people; they landed on the non-accepting side. Ann told me about Darrell's current approach of celibacy – and about a book a guy wrote about celibacy as the way to remain a faithful Christian despite having same-sex attractions.

As I listened to Ann, I remembered my own struggles with my sexuality. How does a sincere believer, a lover of Jesus Christ and the Church, develop a faith that works, while struggling with same-sex desires? A faith amid message after message that if a person were gay, they'd be off the path of Christianity? During my drive home later that night, I thought about how young Darrell must have received those messages. The thoughts made me weep.

My comment back to Ann was, "of course *a* guy wrote *a* book. I think the reason it's *one* guy is because that's pretty close to how many people that strategy works for."

The road of celibacy is wrought with failure and departure. Don't get me wrong, it works for some; those it works for should pursue it if they want. But, if it's the only option for a gay Christian to please God, are most of us are doomed to fail?

In that conversation, this book was born.

Talking with Ann, I shared my story and listened to more of hers. She shared her feelings as a loving parent who only wanted the best for her son. I talked about overcoming my feelings of fear and dread if anyone found out my secret: I was gay.

I wanted to share with her, with Darrell, and with anyone who could use it the love I found in the real, living God.

After my conversation with Ann, I read stories and books about and by gay Christians. While I felt fine about my faith and how it was playing out, I was really interested in what life would be like for a person in the position Darrell had been in. The books presented arguments urging the Church to re-examine its position relating to homosexuality. The authors detailed how people were hurt, turned away, and marginalized when they identified themselves as anything other than straight. One book described how a single Facebook post sympathetic to gay people in the military cost a pastor his position, showing just how sensitive the Christian community can be to the topic of homosexuality.[1] Since then, I've encountered dozens of such stories in print, on social media, and through conversations. They all identify the deep conflict within the believing Christian who loved God and didn't know what to do with their sexuality.

What became clear to me was that we needed a reasonable solution to our problem. If one wasn't presented to us by those telling us we had a problem, we needed to find the solution on our own. It needed to be reliable, successful, and sustainable. We must be able to look ourselves - and God - in the eye, knowing who we are today. We must be able to move forward.

Our challenge was that we came from a faith tradition that believed homosexual behavior was a sin, and we seemed to be drawn very strongly to that behavior. If we went on sinning, many of us thought we weren't saved, and were going to hell. Adding to that fear, every solution proposed by our faith tradition had a track record full of failure. That's what the conservative Christian with same-sex attractions must reconcile.

Much of this book was written during the Covid pandemic, making non-digital resources scarce. Many of the references, as a result, are from digital copies; therefore, the page numbers may not match their printed versions.

TRYING TO BE STRAIGHT

"God loves you and has a wonderful plan for your life!" That's what Laura and I waited in line almost half an hour to say to Heidi Fleiss. It was the first step in sharing the Gospel, or good news, of Jesus Christ, in attempt to win Ms. Fleiss over to our Christian faith. And we were sharing that Gospel with a sexual celebrity.

Heidi Fleiss was "Hollywood's Madam." According to the press and a couple of prosecutors, famous people would pay more than $1,500 for her to arrange an evening of companionship. It was 1994, and she was on the Los Angeles local news every night, on trial for pandering. Front and center was Heidi's threat to expose her little black book, which contained the list of prominent johns who had been her patrons.

Before we got in line, Laura and I passed in front of the underwear store Heidi had set up to offset her legal fees. We were in Old Pasadena, which many of us called Old Town. The area, once a hodgepodge of abandoned buildings and slums, had been revitalized into a bustling mile or so of popular shops, restaurants, and night clubs. The main street, Colorado Boulevard, hosted the Rose Parade each New Year's Day. Old Town was a great place for Heidi to attract foot traffic into her store; coupled with her presence, it created a bit of a fervor – and a line of about 20 people that backed out onto the busy sidewalk.

My friend Laura was a young woman I met in the college ministry at a large evangelical church in Pasadena. She was about 5'3", thin, with shoulder-length brunette hair. Her small stature hid a feisty, voracious attitude. I remember noticing how intense Laura's gaze would get when she would talk about a topic that excited her, matched by the intensity of her voice – not volume, but intensity. Laura had a deep, focused passion for the Gospel and reaching people with it. To me, Laura's energy level and attitude were both attractive and terrifying.

Waiting in the long line of customers, we frantically searched our pockets for Bible tracts – small sized messages carrying God's plan of salvation. We compared four or five options and chose the "Four Spiritual Laws."[1] This was a four-bullet method of winning a non-believer to Christ. We stood in line with people purchasing Heidi's autographed boxers, ready to score one for the Lord.

Heidi was thin, with dark features, and reminded me of Marsha Clark (another notable figure in the 90s). Today I might describe her as a brunette Anne Coulter, if I didn't think it would stir some controversy. I noticed Ms. Fleiss had a relaxed, pleasant way about her as she took her time chatting with the customers whose boxers she signed. She was having a good time meeting her new-found fans.

I thought about what Heidi meant to my world as a sexual person. Emotions of fear and anticipation gripped me. Those days, I did everything I could to avoid my sexual self. The stuff I was ashamed of and hid from my new Christian friends included a lot of experimentation with prostitutes. Had I been richer, would I have been a candidate for Heidi's services?

I was a new believer. I grew up in the Episcopal church but had recently asked God into my life in a different, personal way. I was now a born-again Christian in a conservative, evangelical church. I grappled regularly with my sexual desires. I wasn't alone in that; many men at my church would share privately that they struggled with the "big M" (masturbation) as a problem of lust. The main difference between them and me was while I was attracted to some women, I was really attracted to men.

Instead of dealing with these desires, I created a façade that even I believed. The façade showed that my encounter with Jesus had given me the power and the tools to be a good Christian man who would struggle against and continually overcome sexual temptation. This was the mask I wore when we handed Heidi Fleiss our carefully selected Bible tract, sharing with her the message designed to begin a conversation about the love of God.

Ms. Fleiss was gracious, smiled, thanked us, and said she'd read the miniature pamphlet. We left. And I had cut my first celebrity sex star notch in my evangelist Bible, taking one step away from the reality of my sexuality at the same time.

The intersection of sexuality and the rest of my life scared me. The thought of being found out sometimes made me wonder how I would kill myself if it ever happened. My problem was I had sexual desires that were all over the place – men, women, common household goods; they all played a part in my fantasy life. I was jealous of the people who could just accept their sexualities and live their lives, shunning anyone who disagreed with them. Somehow, I felt I was the exception and couldn't live the life I secretly desired. I wanted a career in the fire service or law enforcement. I wanted respect in conservative Christian institutions. I wanted other people to admire me. I wanted my family to say good things about me when I was away from the dinner table. I figured none of those things were compatible with being gay, or bisexual, or whatever I thought I was.

The result of my fear was to compartmentalize my life – be churchy at church, be conservative at work, be gay with my gay friends, be a normal, well-adjusted adult with my family. The various parts of my life didn't get along very well; most coworkers didn't like to hear about the Bible, my evangelical mega-church wasn't a big fan of gays, and my gay friends weren't too enthusiastic about a church that believed their life-style choices made them an abomination to the Creator of the universe. My family was happy with their faiths, didn't want to hear about mine, and we just didn't talk about sex, ever. There I stood at the intersection, putting up the right façade at the right time, keeping the right things secret, desperately working to be liked and respected by everyone.

Along the way, my passion for reaching others with the hope I had experienced in Jesus grew. People would ask me challenging questions about whether Christianity was true, and I would learn the answers by reading books about Christian apologetics.

Apologetics is the theological discipline of defending the Faith. It's most notably described in 1 Peter 3:15: "Always be prepared to give an answer to everyone who asks you to give the reason for the hope that you have."

I found a university where the writers of those apologetics books taught, so I could work toward my master's degree in

Christian apologetics. Pursuing this degree allowed me to take on more ministry work. I enjoyed teaching. It was a lot of fun to share what I learned – but it came with a price as I was being pulled in two opposite directions with increasing intensity.

I ended up exhausted. I had no idea the toll it was taking on me. The mask I wore while witnessing to Heidi Fleiss stayed on every time I left my apartment, and it came off once a week or so when I could hang out with my gay friends. That was when I could relax and be myself.

THE CHURCH OF BEHAVE

Christianity is a faith founded on grace, love, and mercy. I replaced those fundamentals with an ever-growing set of standards and rules to separate Christians and non-Christians. I accepted the "good news" of God's infinite grace, forgiveness, and love, and then measured its effectiveness with how well I could adhere to the standard of Christian living. Every Sunday I ingested 45-minute sermons based on a passage in the Bible. They were full of theology, instructions on how the verse should be interpreted and applied. Every sermon had a message of God's Grace. Every sermon had a to-do list. I was in the Church of Behave.

Somehow, despite my gay connections, I convinced myself I was straight with a few hiccups. Looking back, it's unbelievable that I bought my own lies – but my rationale was solid. After all, once I was out of the closet, there'd be no going back in. Just like trying to un-ring a bell – the idea of deciding I was straight after announcing I was gay was a no-go.

Being homosexual was frowned upon in evangelical churches (and that's being very generous). That's part of the reason J.P. Moreland gave for signing the recent "Nashville Statement" about homosexuality and gender identity. Dr. Moreland said, "The Bible places great moral weight on a theology and ethics of sexuality, and no single thinker in the history of the church has held that homosexuality, pederasty, bestiality, or sex outside of heterosexual, monogamous marriage is permissible."[2]

Dr. Moreland was my advisor in graduate school, and his recent comments were consistent with the climate I encountered as a grad student of Christian Apologetics at BIOLA University. He's a well-known author in Christian philosophy and apologetics. He's a smart man, and he's not alone. I wanted to impress people like him, and have others see me the way I saw him – a great Christian mind with a solid Christian life.

With the ever-growing public acceptance of non-straight, non-gender conforming people, evangelicals and other conservative religious groups were doubling down on their position. As a result, non-acceptance of homosexual lifestyles has become foundational to the identity of many churches.

Where did that leave a conservative, evangelical fundamentalist like me regarding same-sex desires? I got that repentance was important, but what did repentance look like when it came to my sexuality? There was a tension created between my desire to fit into a community of believers united for the Cause, and the knowledge that a significant part of me was what that cause wanted to see abolished. I wanted to live a life that was pleasing to God but felt I was wholly incapable of the basic life change required for that.

I went to Christian counseling of the "let's not be gay anymore" variety. There, we started with individual sessions with a licensed therapist, followed by group therapy for some. I knew two other guys from my church that went to the same therapist, for the same reason.

Years later, all three of us are still gay. Really, really gay.

Did God love me? Did I love God, or did my lack of a satisfactory sexuality mean I was doing it wrong? Was I just deluding myself and was my love of God fake? And, what about that "wonderful plan for your life" that I'd promised so many others as a faithful witness for Christ? Did God have a wonderful plan for *my* life?

LEARNING TO GROW

Exhausted, confused, frustrated, and convinced the only option I had was to not be gay, I took a break from it all. I moved to the beach while switching jobs and got drunk. I drank a lot. After a while, I was desperate in a way I had never known and hoped to never know again. And while this book isn't about drinking, I must tell you that my trip into a 12-step program wasn't an appealing one.

At the crossroads of despair and hope, I was told the road to hope required me to be completely honest with myself. I was desperate enough to admit that I was gay and figure out what that would mean for my faith later. A couple of years into recovery, I joined a local evangelical church and kept my sexuality to myself. Six years into recovery, at age 43, I joined a new church that accepted everyone, regardless of pretty much anything. That same year, I came out to my parents. Eight years into recovery, I came out to my brother and sister. At twelve years, I introduced my boyfriend to my extended family, friends, and coworkers.

Shortly after joining the recovery program, I eased back into an evangelical, conservative church in San Marcos, California. I had no idea what to do with the sin of homosexuality. I remembered how David was guilty of adultery and murder and was called a "man after God's own heart." Reminding myself that Jesus died for every sin I would ever commit, I was determined to move forward and not worry too much about my sexuality. I kept that all to myself and found ways to be useful. I was in spiritual survival mode, and this worked for several years.

I didn't change one single core belief about the Bible, Jesus, or the Gospel. I completely changed my relationship with God. I finally experienced unconditional Love. God allowed me to know Him in a way I was incapable of before. When I moved to the Bay Area at age 43, I found a new church that allowed me to blossom into my faith in a new way. I had left the Church of Behave and joined the Church of Grow. Trading in a gospel that had morphed into obsession over behavior and performance, I arrived in a church that just didn't care where I was starting from, or where I thought I needed to go. They wanted to support my being and helped me discover a spiritual community that existed to serve God and each other. My new church community challenged me to be a better Christian in ways I had never imagined. I was able to exist in a community that didn't see eye to eye on many issues but committed to struggle together with what it meant to follow Christ.

Today, I can love my family better. When fear comes, I have a place for it. When I screw up, I handle it better. Perhaps the best thing is that I know how to develop compassion for people who anger me – if I'm willing to practice the Christian discipline I've learned through this process.

SEEKING A SOLUTION

What are your options if you're facing the same situations I've faced and emerged from? My path was a bit rockier than what I'd wish upon you. This book presents a few alternatives and discusses their ups and downs.

To understand and build our solutions, it's helpful to know how conservative Christians build their practice of faith. After all, if we were looking to leave the faith, this book wouldn't be of any interest to you the reader or me as a writer. We could just leave and do something else. There's something that keeps us wanting to stay in this community, even though some in that community tell us we're not welcome (or at least that God isn't happy with us).

I began my Christian walk believing the Bible was clear that homosexuality was a sin, and to reconcile anything other than traditional sexual mores meant to become a liberal and throw out the Bible. I would dismiss statements made by liberal theologians before I heard them. Marcus Borg, an influential participant in the liberal "Jesus Seminar" was one of these scholars. If Marcus had recommended a good burger, I would have gone out for tacos.

So that's in my mind when I'm writing this book. My intention is to write this from the conservative perspective – because it's not my desire to change your core beliefs, criticize your church, or berate someone who has made a positive impact on your life. If you want to do that yourself, have at it. As for me, I'm writing to help you figure out your side of the street. To do that, I'll quote as many conservatives as I can. Using a conservative approach to faith and the Scriptures, we can understand options for living a God-honoring life that aren't necessarily in the conservative's playbook.

A lot of you will hopefully see value in finding a way to grow in your relationship with God – and that will mean finding a healthy, effective way of addressing your sexuality. To do that, there are a few tools that are helpful in your spiritual toolbox. The first is to develop a solid understanding of the Gospel and common pitfalls that pull believers away from it. Second, is to build the same kind of understanding as it relates to reading and interpreting the Bible. This would include some work around the six passages that are purported to address homosexuality. With the Gospel and Holy Scriptures in mind, a believer can identify a course of action based on where they are now, and where they want to be. With a solid understanding of the Christian Gospel and how conservatives typically interpret Scriptures, we can explore some options in how homosexuality, both desires and behavior, can be reconciled through a healthy relationship with God.

You may not want or need to leave your church. You might want to run for the hills and give church a break for a while. You may search out another church where you can be more yourself and still grow. This book will help you if you love Jesus, the Bible, and want to reconcile that love with desires you may find inescapable.

This book will take us through the Gospel and point out where we can use it to help us down whatever path we've chosen to walk. We will explore the various concepts behind how the Bible is best understood, while considering the opinions of the very people who seek to keep us out of their churches as we are today. We'll look at options for how to move forward as Christians, free to grow and serve as God intended for each one of us.

My goal isn't to win you over to my way of living or my way of thinking. It's to help you develop a way to live that you can live with. A faith that works. A vibrant relationship with God through Jesus Christ.

COMING TO TERMS

"FOR A STRAIGHT GUY, I SURE DO SLEEP WITH A LOT OF MEN!"

I remember that thought running through my head in my mid-twenties. I didn't understand how hilarious that thought was until years later.

While telling myself the story that I was just a misaligned straight guy, I overlooked the fear lurking inside me. It was an uneasiness I felt in my belly – from the knowledge that coming out to myself or anyone else would be unretractable and bad. That realization made it easy to believe my own lie.

Not labeling myself gay allowed me a certain degree of arrogance toward those who had; I hadn't given up the fight against my sexuality. That put me, in my mind, a step above the people who had come out and succumbed to what were, in my opinion, ungodly desires.

My secret friends in various gay neighborhoods (I liked to call them "gayborhoods") around Los Angeles provided me an escape where I could relax and be myself. The tension between my ideal life and my real life increased the longer this went on. While alcohol removed some of that tension, it didn't solve my problem.

How I labeled myself was important. Labels helped me avoid facing my biggest dilemmas. I wasn't an alcoholic; I was just a heavy drinker. I wasn't gay; I was bisexual at worst, or straight (depending on my mood at the time). It felt better to hide behind my not-so-bad rationalizations than deal with the conditions that drove me toward these behaviors.

I entered my 30s with two problems: my drinking and my sexuality. Only when I was able to look my drinking in the eye and recognize what it was could I deal with it effectively. The same held true for my sexuality – but with different results.

When I was ready to be done with drinking, I broke down and asked God for help. I surrendered to a program that allowed me to act in faith, asking for God's power to help me stop. It's been working for a while now. Not drinking and a systematic process of spiritual growth made my life much better than it was.

I had a similar approach to my sexuality. I broke down and asked God for help. I surrendered to a program of Christian reparative counseling recommended by a large para-church ministry.

My life got worse.

Applying the idea to deny myself in terms of my sexuality only hid the problem. That led to other problems that could only be solved by un-denying myself and being honest about who I was. It turned out that being gay was part of what made me 'me.' The ultimatum that finally changed my life for the better was either accept myself for who I was or go back to the downward spiral of misery that drinking brought with it.

While a Christ-based approach to change my drinking solved my problem, a Christ-based approach to change my sexuality did not.

How we label ourselves is important. It determines who we see when we look in the mirror, how we treat ourselves, and how we treat others. Until I faced myself as a gay man, I couldn't take the necessary steps to make that work in my life – both in practical matters and in my faith as a Christian.

WHO AM I?

If you Google "gay and Christian," you'll find lots of pages dedicated to convincing you such people don't exist, with variations on the following thoughts:

- It's a sin, and sin is incompatible with a Christian identity
- Our identity is in Christ, not in our sexualities
- It's a choice, not an identity
- It's a behavior, not an identity
- It's an attraction, not an identity
- Being gay is a made-up concept; there are no such things as gay people[1]

I find the idea of identity versus a characteristic, flaw, or quality intriguing. Speaking with one Christian psychologist, I was quickly corrected when I used the term "gay" to describe someone who didn't identify as such but had exclusively same-sex desires.

WHAT'S ON YOUR NAME TAG?

In his book *How to Win Friends and Influence People*, Dale Carnegie spends an entire chapter on the importance of remembering someone's name.[2] Our names are the first stop on the way toward our identities.

Can you imagine what your church would be like if everyone wore name tags? Well, mine does. It's great for a guy like me. I constantly feel insecure remembering the names of people I've known for years, so glancing down at their nametag allows me to feel better about getting it right.

Our name tags are important because we serve each other communion by name. First, the priest comes around with the bread, saying, "Andy, the body of Christ." Then, one of my fellow parishioners hands me the chalice of wine, saying, "Andy, the blood of Christ."

After that, it's my turn. Chalice in hand, I turn to the person next to me, and use their name. It's special. We look each other in the eye while this is happening. We are connected to each other, celebrating Jesus' sacrifice and the hope He offers.

Can you imagine if our name tags all read, "Christian"? That's what I believe many suggest when they say our identity isn't gay, or straight, but instead simply "Christian."

When Paul speaks of stripping away our identities, it's usually in the context of divisions. He writes in Galatians 3:28,

> So in Christ Jesus you are all children of God through faith, for all of you who were baptized into Christ have clothed yourselves with Christ. There is neither Jew nor Gentile, neither slave nor free, nor is there male and female, for you are all one in Christ Jesus.

When we look at this verse in the context of Galatians, we find that Paul was urging the church not to divide between Jews and Gentiles. He made that point in several ways supporting a bigger idea concerning freedom from the law.

Put another way: As the result of their identity in Christ, how many devout Christians wake up in the morning and say, "I'm not a man or woman, I'm a Christian!"?

If we truly were to deny these identities, many of the same conservatives telling us not to identify as gay, but rather as Christians, would have to revisit the reasons they divide between men and women in church leadership roles; while being gay isn't specifically mentioned in this passage as an identity, male and female is!

Who we are in Christ is a real thing. Who we are as individual people is also a real thing. Paul is advising us against using these parts of our identities to divide our churches, which is exactly what a church does when it puts gays in a separate class of membership.

Take Luke for example. Luke was a physician. In addition to finding that referenced in other parts of the New Testament, there is medical language in Luke's Gospel. So, while Luke's Gospel was God-inspired (literally, "God-breathed"), Luke the physician was still Luke, the physician.

What I've always taken from that is the Holy Spirit preserves our identities. He allows us to be who we really are and become our truest selves through God's grace and mercy. Now as believers, indwelt by God's Holy Spirit, we have an opportunity to understand and become our real selves.

BE CAREFUL WHAT YOU CALL YOURSELF

The late comedian George Carlin was good with words. A lot of his comedy centered around the meanings of words and terms. One routine I remember was his analysis of the term "shell shock:"

> When people can't handle any more combat - in the First World War, that was called shell shock, which is very simple, honest and direct language... In the Second World War, a generation later, they decided to call that battle fatigue. It's twice as long now, four syllables, takes longer to say, doesn't seem to hurt. Fatigue is a nicer word than shock...
>
> Then we had Korea in 1950. They called the same thing operational exhaustion. Now that humanity is completely missing from it and it sounds like something that might happen to your jeep. And in Vietnam, of course, the same condition was called post-traumatic stress disorder. And my point is, if we had still been calling it shell shock, maybe Vietnam veterans might have gotten some attention at the time.[3]

When I think about how we as Christians label our sexuality, I think of Carlin's "Shell Shock" routine.

Many leaders in the ex-gay movement have allowed us to avoid the harsh reality of who we are by re-labeling us. Some say we're "same-sex attracted." Others say we're "suffering from unwanted same-sex attractions." Still others have labeled being gay as "same-sex attachment disorder."[4]

It should get our attention that something as simple as being gay has been relabeled to the point that it sounds like a skin condition. We can see the impact of this later when we look at the various conversion therapy techniques that have been developed under the assumptions driven by such labels.

Why not just be gay? Or lesbian? Or bisexual? We need to be careful about the stories we tell ourselves about ourselves, lest we miss giving that part of ourselves the attention it needs.

THE NAMES PEOPLE PLAY

Lesbian, Gay, Bisexual, Transgender, Queer, Questioning, Intersex, Asexual, and everyone else who's not straight by the strictest standard. The most out there LGBTQQIA+ people I know call the acronyms that describe the non-hetero, non-cisgender world "alphabet soup" with a chuckle. So where do I, and more importantly, where do you fall in that soup? Thinking of these terms, I prefer "gay" to describe myself.

I sometimes slip and use that term to include lesbians, bisexuals, and maybe even the entire gamut of what used to be called "alternative sexualities."[5] Occasionally, a friend will call me out on it. "I'm lesbian, not gay," is a good example. The challenge to me is that I never know what anyone wants to be called until I ask them.

These distinctions are important. Waking up in the morning and finding myself attracted to guys is different than waking up in the morning and realizing that the gender I identify with differs from what my parents may have defined for me.

I'm writing this book to Christians who are attracted to people of the same sex in one way or another. Some of them identify as men, others as women, and still others as neither, or a non-binary combination of the two. I don't know how you refer to yourself, and it's important that I get it right.

There are also many who will read this book and insist that

while they have same-sex attractions, they don't identify as gay. If that's you, please know that I respect that and find it to be a perfectly valid option for you to choose.

At the same time, there are those who recoil at the term "same-sex attracted." They associate it with a traumatic conversion therapy, family, or church experience they'd wish to leave behind. To them, same-sex attracted, or SSA, represents self-loathing. Just the term will drive some to adrenaline laden panic and depression – which is why I avoid it for the most part in this book.

A Facebook group I'm in centered around survivors of conversion therapy blew up the other day when a Black member used the term "same-gender loving." A few people in the group reacted negatively as the term was so close to "same-sex attracted." As the majority of the group were white men, we were clueless to know that "same-gender loving" was a term created in the 1990s by African Americans because the language around LGBTQ people then was white-centric and failed to encompass the Black gay experience.

Writing this book to all of the above, the challenge is to use terms that people can identify with and not offend. Since that may not be possible, readers may need to set aside some of the visceral responses that come with some of these terms.

I invite you to self-translate terms that offend into terms you can better identify with.

WHY I THINK WE'RE ALL GAY

We're not all gay. However, there is no term or set of terms I can use that will be unoffensive to anyone who has a horse in this race. We need a way to get around our labels and hit something that goes deeper than a word or a term.

This book mostly uses the terms "gay" and refers to same-sex relationships to encompass the wide variety of expressions to describe anyone "not straight." It is my desire to fully affirm how you recognize yourself today, and how you recognize yourself as you want to be. My challenge to you as a reader is to look past some terminology you don't feel comfortable with so as to interact with the ideas and solutions we'll discuss.

Those solutions can start with a hard look at Scripture, the Gospel, and the alternatives our church leaders have identified to our "alternative lifestyles" (as they've labeled them). After that, we can start to plot a course through which we can grow as God's people.

A FAITH THAT WORKS: CAN GOD CURE ME?

Is there a tool in the Christian faith or otherwise that will work to help me not be gay anymore? Many of us have looked to some form of conversion therapy, including the Ex-Gay movement, for an answer. The idea should be simple: God objects to homosexuality; God frees believers from things He objects to; therefore, God should free believers from homosexuality.

We need a faith that works. Many of us look to our faith to help us work out our sexuality. And if God can make us not gay anymore, it solves our problem of being gay and Christian!

What I mean by "faith that works" is faith that functions as it's supposed to. That brings me again to Dr. J.P. Moreland, my graduate school advisor.

I have always liked Dr. Moreland. I enjoyed listening to and reading his work. In his approach to faith, he seemed to buy some of the things other apologists scoffed at. One such position Dr. Moreland wasn't bashful about was saying, "I'm a mystic," meaning he believed God still performed supernatural miracles. These were things that challenged me and made me think.

One night, I attended an apologetics event with a couple of speakers. It was the first time I had the opportunity to hear Dr. Moreland speak live. One thing he said really gave me pause. He said, "if you're not a Christian, why not try it for a year? If it doesn't work, you can always quit."

I thought, "that's real faith – he believes it so strongly he's willing to use the fact that Christianity works as its own convincing argument!"

Dr. Moreland wasn't saying, "If this works, it must be true." That would have gone against his and others' teachings. Just because something works doesn't mean its claims are true. Instead, he was saying, "if it's true, it ought to work."

I've come to appreciate that about Christianity. Our faith ought to work in practical ways; if it doesn't, we need to reevaluate how we apply our beliefs. This includes how my sexuality intersects my relationship with God.

If God sent Jesus so we could have a successful relationship with Him and we do what's required on our end to engage that relationship, then any remaining barriers should be removed. We can expect a solution to any problem that would come between us and our loving Creator, based on His promise (Rom 8:38).

SEXUAL ORIENTATION CHANGE EFFORTS

Many Christians struggling with their sexuality look for a cure. That's not a surprise - many of us have pre-programmed responses to homosexuality as being undesirable. It makes sense, then, that there is an industry to meet that desire to change.

The effort to change one's sexuality has many names and continues to evolve. You can find it under sexual orientation change efforts (SOCE), conversion therapy, reparative therapy, certain applications of EMDR (an eye-movement therapy for trauma survivors), and numerous non-therapeutic support groups in organizations such as churches. There are some licensed professionals who engage in SOCE, and several para-church ministries who do so, who are not necessarily licensed or certified in the practice. Until recently, many participants in the movements associated with SOCE called themselves "Ex-gay."

When answering the question, "Can we be cured?" we need a reliable solution to our situation: We're experiencing gay desires in a religious tradition that condemns people with gay desires. Politics, ideologies, left-wing, right-wing...all need to take a back seat to our primary need to take care of ourselves while we develop an approach to our sexuality and our faith that works.

THE BIRTH OF CHRISTIAN CONVERSION THERAPY

In 1973, the American Psychiatric Association removed "homo-sexuality" from its list of diagnosable conditions in the DSM-IV, the *Diagnostic and Statistical Manual of Mental Disorders*. It was a major turn for gays, and a major thorn for many conservatives, especially Christian organizations.

The impetus for changing the DSM diagnosis came largely from a study done by Dr. Evelyn Hooker in the 1950s. Dr. Hooker compared the mental health characteristics of hetero-sexual men and an equal number of avowed, "out" homosexual men. She put in place controls to ensure the men were on equal footing in age, education, and IQ. Outside scholars and critics were unable to use the results to identify who was gay and who was straight – the difference in mental health between the two groups was indistinguishable.[1]

Homosexuality could no longer be attributed to the cause or effect of "impairment in judgment, reliability or general social and vocational capabilities"; it did not belong as a mental disorder.[2]

About the same time as the DSM change, the first notable modern conversion therapy organization grew out of a hippie outreach church just north of San Francisco. A local pastor named Kent Philpott wrote a book called *The Third Sex?* that presented six case-studies of homosexuals who had been "freed." The book showed how all six subjects successfully navigated out of the "homosexual lifestyle," with five subjects no longer considering themselves homosexual, and one committed to celibacy.[3]

The cover of the book proclaimed, "These six stories of how homosexuals were changed through Christ will help save your children." People came flocking to the North Bay to experience the same freedom as the six examples in the book. Riding the wave of interest in this newfound solution, Philpott, with John Evans and Frank Worthen, founded Love in Action. Love in Action continued as a residential program for decades. It was featured in films such as *This is What Love in Action Looks Like* and *Boy Erased*.

Meanwhile, an ex-gay group in Anaheim had started a telephone hotline and ministry called EXIT. The hotline allowed people wanting freedom from homosexuality a place to call for support.

EXIT, with some help from Frank Worthen and Love in Action, formed Exodus International. Exodus International was a network of ex-gay ministries that were mostly Christian. It became the largest, longest running ex-gay organization to date.

Since that time, dozens, if not hundreds of Christian and other religious-based organizations have been created. Many of them joined with Exodus International to form a network for growth in their programs.

DOES IT WORK?

When I first thought about reparative or conversion therapy, I understood the two founders of Exodus International had run off with each other. While slightly inaccurate, my reaction was to think that gay conversion therapy probably didn't work.

Why, then, did I spend three years of my time, energy, and money in reparative therapy?

Desperation and disgust.

When I had had an all-night encounter with a man I'd met online, and no time to sleep before a date with a woman from the college group at church, I broke. Besides being exhausted, I was disgusted with myself and intensely afraid of what my sexuality meant for me. If I didn't do something, I was afraid I'd have to leave my ministries, all of which I loved. Afraid I'd never have that dream life I was supposed to want – the wife and kids, the nice house, the supportive church community I read about in the Bible and saw in some of the groups at my church. I was ready to accept whatever I needed to do – to get right with Jesus and myself.

I knew another man at my church who was in therapy for

sexual issues, and I got a referral to a therapist named Rick. During our first meeting, I told Rick my concern, "I don't want to blame this on my parents. That seems like a copout."

Rick replied, "Okay, if you ever feel like that's what we're doing, please tell me."

Rick was a pleasant, reserved guy. Looking to be in his early forties. The way he talked, the way he sat, all reminded me of some of the affectations ex-gay ministries tried to correct in their programs (like the "masculine" and "feminine" ways to cross one's legs while seated). I knew Rick was married and knew he had a kid. I never had the guts to ask him if he had dealt with his own sexuality.

During our time together, we talked a lot about what life was like growing up. We talked about the messages I received as a kid, and I began to draw connections between conflicts I had as a teen and experiences as a small child, even as a toddler and infant. I finally had a connection between my sexuality as the effect of my relationship with my parents – especially my dad.

As enlightening as that was, there were two issues. First, knowing the cause, if my relationship with my parents really was the cause, didn't do anything to change the effect. I still had every desire, drive, and impulse I had when we started. Second, just because we talked about some very real issues with my parents didn't mean those issues had anything to do with any of my sexual desires.

Conversion therapy was my last hope of not being this way. The result of three years of therapy was no change whatsoever.

BUT DOES IT WORK?

Almost 50 years of Christian organizations helping God change gays should have a measurable result, don't you think? Here's what John Smid said after 22 years of running Love in Action:

> People would ask us about our success rate…And I would say 'Well, our real goal is to lead people to have a better relationship with God. And everyone that goes through LIA, they have a better relationship with God. So I would say that's a pretty good success rate.' Because underneath it, I was afraid to say, we haven't seen anyone change…[4]

Studies should play a role in developing our approach to our decision concerning therapy. The challenge is finding one that supports the effectiveness of changing our orientation through therapy.

Recently, work produced by Cornell University examined 47 peer-reviewed studies regarding whether conversion therapy can be effective without causing harm. Of the 47 studies:

> 12 concluded that [conversion therapy] is ineffective and/or harmful, finding links to depression, suicidality, anxiety, social isolation and decreased capacity for intimacy. Only one study concluded that sexual orientation change efforts could succeed — although only in a minority of its participants, and the study has several limitations: its entire sample self-identified as religious and it is based on self-reports, which can be biased and unreliable. The remaining 34 studies do not make an empirical determination about whether [conversion therapy] can alter

sexual orientation but may offer useful observations to help guide practitioners who treat LGB patients.[5]

The one study supporting the conclusion, above, that SOCE could be effective was performed by Dr. Joseph Nicolosi, the founder of NARTH, the National Association for Research and Treatment of Homosexuality. The problem of course, was NARTH was a professional organization dedicated to promoting conversion therapy, which may make their study a bit suspect.

THE CHRISTIAN EX-GAY MOVEMENT: FAILURE, FRAUD, AND FORNICATION

You'll know a tree by its fruit. Jesus tells us that in Matthew, Chapter 7. I try to be a good fruit, and so should you. What fruits do we see when we look at the ex-gay movement?

Perhaps we can look at the results of the faith-based programs as a whole? A movement that began in the 1970s should surely have a track record.

Here's a timeline:

1973: Four of the six stories in *The Third Sex* were contested by the people they were about as falsehoods. The book that started the Christian movement in SOCE was removed from circulation as a result.

1979: Founding member of Exodus International Michael Bussee and volunteer Gary Cooper fell in love with each other. They left their wives and later had a wedding ceremony.[6]

1986: Homosexuals Anonymous founder Colin Cook resigned after an investigation revealed a pattern of inappropriate sexual conduct with clients.[7]

2000: After working for The SALT (The Saviors Alliance for

Lifting the Truth) and Americans for Truth About Homosexuality to share with the nation he had been cured from being gay, 21-year-old Wade Richards publicly recanted his story. A graduate of Love in Action's residential program in Tennessee, Wade maintained he remained gay the whole time.[8]

2000: John Paulk, who had been featured on the cover of *Newsweek* as proof that gays can change, was photographed leaving a gay bar in Washington D.C. He later admitted there had been no change in his sexuality. At the time he was photographed, Paulk worked for Focus on the Family, running their gender and homosexuality division, and was the chair of the board of directors for Exodus International.[9]

2003: Michael Johnston was the founder of "National Coming Out of Homosexuality Day" and a television ad model for several ex-gay Christian organizations with the message, "A decade ago I walked away from homosexuality through the power of Jesus Christ." In 2003, Michael was accused of spreading HIV to men he met online. He reportedly did not disclose his HIV status to those men.[10]

2007: Richard Cohen, author of *Coming Out Straight: Understanding and Healing Homosexuality* and board president for Parents and Friends of Ex Gays and Gays (PFOX) demonstrated techniques used to heal homosexuality in three national television forums. His performance on the *Daily Show with John Stewart* made a mockery of ex-gay therapies. These included male holding, where he cuddled with his clients. After the show, Richard was quickly and quietly removed from his positions. Prior to this, organizations such as NARTH marketed his materials and had reportedly applauded similar demonstrations with Cohen as a speaker at their conventions.[11]

2008: Amid a slew of public protest and controversy, John

Smid resigned as the director of Love In Action. He married his same-sex partner in 2014.[12] John's role was later portrayed in the movie *Boy Erased*, as the character Victor Sykes played by Joel Edgerton. John was a special consultant for the film.[13]

2010: George Rekers, a founder of the Family Research Council, and on the board of directors for NARTH, was discovered taking a vacation with a male prostitute he met on Rentboy.com, a website that has been since shut down by the FBI due to it being a vehicle for prostitution. Rekers stated he hired the young man to carry his luggage.[14]

2012: Jews Offering New Alternatives to Homosexuality (JONAH) was sued for consumer fraud – later found liable by a New Jersey court and forced to close its doors. CNN reported:

> The conversion therapy techniques included having them strip naked in group sessions, cuddling and intimate holding of others of the same-sex, violently beating an effigy of their mothers with a tennis racket, visiting bath houses 'in order to be nude with father figures,' and being 'subjected to ridicule as "faggots" and "homos" in mock locker room scenarios,' the suit said.[15]

2012: Robert Spitzer recanted his 2003 study that indicated peoples' orientations could be changed by therapy. Spitzer's study had been the only study showing the possibility of change outside of the ex-gay movement itself.[16]

2013: Exodus International, the largest, longest-running ex-gay organization in the world, announced it would close. Director Alan Chambers issued an apology to the gays and ex-gays the organization had condemned and disillusioned over its years.[17] He also made several public statements that while the therapy his organization provided helped some, it also hurt many, and didn't work to "cure" homosexuals.[18]

2014: *The Post and Courier* summarized, "In 2014, nine founders and leaders from some of the country's most prominent programs and ministries wrote an open letter calling for a nationwide ban on the practice [of conversion therapy]. The letter was published online by the National Center for Lesbian Rights."[19]

2019: David Matheson, author of *Becoming a Whole Man* and co-founder of the ex-gay ministry "Journey into Manhood" left his wife and announced he will pursue a male-male relationship. He has been described as an "early protégé of Dr. Joseph Nicolosi" and an "intellectual godfather of conversion therapy."[20]

2019: McKrae Game, after 20 years as the founder and director of the ex-gay ministry Hope for Wholeness, came out publicly. He stated that conversion therapy is a "lie," "very harmful," and "false advertising."[21]

Here are some notable quotes from former ex-gay leaders:

Yvette Cantu Schneider, former director of women's ministry at Exodus International, speaker at Focus on the Family's "Love Won Out" campaign:

> I was the director of women's ministry for Exodus International. You know what I spent my time doing? Dealing with leaders in 'ex-gay' ministries who were having sex with the people who were coming to them for help. And that's when I knew if the leaders, the people who have been chosen to be leaders, aren't changing, no one is changing. [22]

John Smid, director at Love in Action for 22 years:

As I look back to my own 22-year history as an 'ex-gay' leader featured on programs such as ABC's 20/20, I can now say that I was swindled into believing I could change. In so doing, I subsequently deceived many because of my own inability to be honest with myself. I continued to solicit clients and donations for our ministry with a watered-down message that somehow God was providing the miracle of change.[23]

John Paulk, founder of Focus on the Family's "Love Won Out" program, North American director at Exodus International, and co-author of "Love Won Out: How God's Love Helped Two People Leave Homosexuality and Find Each Other":

Please allow me to be clear: I do not believe that reparative therapy changes sexual orientation; in fact, it does great harm to many people.

I know that countless people were harmed by things I said and did in the past. Parents, families, and their loved ones were negatively impacted by the notion of reparative therapy and the message of change. I am truly, truly sorry for the pain I have caused.[24]

McKrae Game, founder and director of Hope for Wholeness:

I was a religious zealot that hurt people. People said they attempted suicide over me and the things I said to them. People, I know, are in therapy because of me. Why would I want that to continue?[25]

Michael Bussee, co-founder of Exodus International:

No one was really becoming 'ex-gay.' Who were we fooling? As one current EXODUS leader admitted, we were just 'Christians with homosexual tendencies who would rather not have those tendencies.' By calling ourselves 'ex-gay' we were lying to ourselves and to others. We were hurting people.[26]

Finally, Alan Chambers, director of Exodus International:

> Please know that I am deeply sorry. I am sorry for the pain and hurt many of you have experienced. I am sorry that some of you spent years working through the shame and guilt you felt when your attractions didn't change. I am sorry we promoted sexual orientation change efforts and reparative theories about sexual orientation that stigmatized parents...
>
> More than anything, I am sorry that so many have interpreted this religious rejection by Christians as God's rejection. I am profoundly sorry that many have walked away from their faith and that some have chosen to end their lives...[27]

I hope you've paid close attention to the above quotes and special attention to *who* was saying them. Every organization has its critics. Every movement has its flaws. This, however, is different. These are key leaders, founders, and posterchildren of significant organizations within the conversion therapy movement, many funded and supported by major Christian organizations.

While those remaining in the movement continue to rebrand and morph their programs into more likable terms, the number of ex-gay leaders walking away claiming fraud is astonishing. The number of people featured in nationwide media who never changed is astonishing. The fact that these ministries and organizations seemed to take these failures in stride is disappointing.

SHOULD I GO INTO THERAPY?

Even with the overwhelming volume of stories showing SOCE is ineffective, a few still hold to the old Exodus motto, "Change is Possible." While Alan Chambers apologizes for the failures of Exodus, he does so while married to a woman, and reports that he's happy.

UCLA's Williams Institute maintains a study that estimates 698,000 American adults have been through conversion therapy. Allen Chambers' story is but one of those.

When I look at current groups of people claiming success through SOCE, two things stick out. First, there are typically a couple dozen people excited enough to wave their proverbial flag. Second, there's not a lot of gray hair in that crowd!

Many participants, including me, experienced little or no change in their sexual attractions and desires despite trying really, really hard in various programs and therapies. There are people no longer with us who wrote suicide notes explaining that their failure to please God through their sexuality was what drove them to that decision. It's also impossible to ignore the former leaders and founders of the ex-gay movement and its various organizations who repeatedly claim it never worked.

From a commonsense standpoint, and from discussing conversion therapy with both its proponents and opponents, I can't recommend conversion therapy to anyone I care about. What would I say to the person who is still bent on going to therapy? Manage your expectations wisely with these facts in mind:

1. The ex-gay movement has a history of repeated

failures at all levels, with a long list of resignations and apologies by its leaders.

2. The secular side of the SOCE movement has given up the goal of conversion.

3. An overwhelming number of psychiatric organizations have come out against reparative or conversion therapies as either ineffective or harmful.

4. There is no standardized set of therapies or requirements for certification in religious SOCE programs.

5. There is no standardized or recognized set of therapies for SOCE in licensed settings.

6. The therapies currently in use have no established success rate.

One thing I've heard from many church leaders, and Dr. Moreland as well (in so many words): If God's in it, it will work. I don't think God's "in it" when it comes to conversion therapy.

We'll need a better solution than SOCE if we're betting our souls on our success!

CELIBACY

You can't have illicit sex if you're not having sex.

That's simple. We could extend that to relationships as well by saying you can't be in an inappropriate romantic relationship if you avoid romantic relationships altogether. If you remain convinced that God's message to the world includes "don't be gay," and you're not heading toward conversion therapy, you'll need a way to comply. Celibacy could be your answer.

Many Christians who struggle with their sexuality decide the best approach is to remain celibate. Celibacy is practiced by many denominations within Christianity – most notably by Roman Catholics who enter the priesthood. The concept exists in Scripture. Celibacy was lauded by Jesus, as well as Paul, as preferable to marriage:

Matthew 19:11-12 says,

Jesus replied, 'Not everyone can accept this word, but only those to whom it has been given. For there are eunuchs who were born that way, and there are eunuchs who have been made eunuchs by others—and there are those who choose to live like eunuchs for the sake of the kingdom of heaven. The one who can accept this should accept it.'

Paul says to the Corinthians in 1 Cor 7:8-9,

Now to the unmarried and the widows I say: It is good for them to stay unmarried, as I do. But if they cannot control themselves, they should marry, for it is better to marry than to burn with passion.

I've heard Christians talk about celibacy as a gift. Many Christian authors suggest celibacy in one form or another as an appropriate response to same-sex attractions.

I like to compare the idea of celibacy as a "gift" that comes with our sexualities with the exciting night of trick-or-treating from when I was young. We were on the hunt for the best candy in our neighborhood – armed with the biggest pillowcases we owned, to fill as much as we could. We approached one house, and a group of kids leaving told us, "Don't bother with this one – the guy must be a dentist. He gave us toothbrushes!"

A lot of churches, church leaders, and religious folk tell us if we can't marry a person of the opposite sex, we should embrace the gift of celibacy. Those people are like the guy handing out toothbrushes on Halloween– except with celibacy, it's like being told we can only visit the toothbrush guy, while we watch all our friends going to the other houses with candy. They would come home with bags full of candy, and we would have the consolation from our parents that healthy teeth are important; the toothbrush was really the better Halloween find.

Christopher Yuan wrote *Holy Sexuality*.[1] Yuan's book advocates abstinence from sexual desires that go against what he calls "God's plan for sexuality," and urges Christians to leave the door open to wedding an opposite sex partner. He differentiated between desires and attractions, so we could draw a line in our minds between an innocent, sinless attraction and that attraction growing wings and becoming a sinful desire.

I paid attention to Yuan's work for a couple of reasons. First, he's one of us, having come out of a tumultuous life of gay relationships (while his drug use, crime, and prison history may not align with most of our stories). Second, he's over 40. Have you noticed how many 26-year-olds write about the amazing success they've had with celibacy? There's potential for us to learn from Dr. Yuan about what he calls a life of singleness from his sustained experience.

Yuan says we should measure our desires based on where they would lead us if we were to act on them. Thus, even romantic, non-sexual same-sex desires are wrong in Yuan's view. To play this out, one would need to choose between desiring marriage to a person of the opposite sex or a life of being single. As important, Yuan says we must regulate our desires to align with that plan – not to allow our attractions to become inappropriate desires. Yuan believes that intimacy and communion for the single person should be found in the church as a spiritual family.[2]

Another author and champion for celibacy is Wesley Hill. Hill describes his realization in high school that God affirmed marriage between a man and woman while forbidding any other sexual intimacy. According to Hill, as a gay Christian, he must either marry a woman or remain celibate.[3]

Hill's solution is to cultivate and renew friendship as the place for that meaningful form of intimacy and communion with another person. This could include a same-sex relationship that is non-romantic and not sexual.

While Yuan believes calling oneself gay is inappropriate for Christian believers because our identity should be in Christ, Hill identifies himself as gay while avoiding certain behaviors that would fall into that category. Both authors identify a significant problem that comes with a celibate or single lifestyle. The problem has little to do with sex. Hill writes:

> My primary question, over time, became a question about love. Where was I to find love? Where was I to give love? If Scripture and the Christian tradition were right that I shouldn't try to find a husband, surely the apparent corollary couldn't also be right—that I was therefore cut off from any deep, meaningful form of intimacy and communion. Could it?[4]

Along the same path, Christopher Yuan advocates celibate Christians find a spiritual family. In reaching his vision for a spiritual family, Yuan correctly identifies a problematic church culture that is based on the married family unit. As such, most churches place singleness in a category of a temporary problem that needs to be solved:

You may be thinking, what does a deficient view of single-ness have to do with my gay loved one? A lot. Since it's God's will for her or him to refrain from same-sex relationships, being single would be a part of their reality now and possibly much longer. Are our church communities a vibrant place for these singles to grow and thrive in their Christian faith? Let's be honest: not really.[5]

I remember the first time I experienced this attitude at church. I was 25 and a few months into my faith as a born-again believer. A guest preacher gave the sermon, and after the service I went up to meet him and thank him for coming. The man had a great passion for reaching people for Jesus. I was excited to talk to him about his sermon and eager to share that I was a new believer. Before I could ask my first question, he asked me "Andy, are you married?"

I told the preacher I was single, and he began praying that God would send me a good woman to be my wife. That was it; we parted ways with me puzzled over why he thought this was the one issue in my newly found faith that I needed to focus on.

Over time, it became clear that ministries for young adults, even if they didn't orient themselves toward hitching people, were places to do just that. Marriage was – and still is – an important goal for the modern Christian.

The second issue Yuan addresses is the difficulty in developing platonic male relationships:

Many Christian men are deathly afraid to build a godly friendship with a same-sex-attracted Christian brother for fear that it might become inappropriate.[6]

The spiritual family Christopher Yuan identifies as a replacement for marriage could be a wonderful thing. The challenge is that most people don't attend church for a spiritual family – they attend for the service, the teaching, or the youth group to either start or support their family.

While the ideal of finding spiritual friendship or a spiritual family is appealing, it may not be available to us, and may not work as a substitute for the kind of love people seek in romantic relationships and marriage.

THE ALTERNATIVE TO SINGLENESS

Let's look at 1 Corinthians 7:8-9 again:

> Now to the unmarried and the widows I say: It is good for them
> to stay unmarried, as I do. But if they cannot control
> themselves, they should marry, for it is better to marry than to
> burn with passion.

What about marrying if you burn with passion? A few people who don't burn with passion and identify as having same-sex attractions have told us how wonderful it is to be single, celibate, spiritual friends, or whatever else. The problem is, of course, it's seemingly just a few people with that experience. Many of us have a really hard time with it. What do we do if we can't handle celibacy and singleness?

A person or organization should be able to follow their own standards for me to take them seriously. The leaders of the movements who tell us to stay single by and large discourage singleness for everyone else in their congregations.

People in our churches who point to Paul's admonition about singleness and celibacy don't follow it. If they did, we'd see lots of single people in church, and it would be celebrated. If you're one of the people who burns with passion, you still have a problem; while straight people who burn have an out (marriage), it doesn't involve celibacy. If that's the case, celibacy might not work for you.

The scriptural issue with celibacy as a solution for gays in the church is there seems to be a missing solution for those who burn with passion. If you're one of those folks who can't seem to make celibacy work, you've got a fair complaint.

We need a solution that works. We need not be surprised when a solution that doesn't work for any other part of the church doesn't necessarily work for us!

SINGLENESS: BLESSING OR CURSE?

There are benefits to being single. I spent much of my adult life by myself, and it allowed me to explore hobbies and ministries a married person with a family might have missed. I got my pilot's license, learned how to windsurf, and even competed internationally (poorly, I might add). I ran sound for a local Christian ska band, went to grad school, dabbled in amateur (Ham) radio, joined my local volunteer fire department, and the list continues to grow. All these hobbies would probably take a back seat to driving kids to soccer practice if I had the "normal" life of a straight married man.

While I've seen and experienced much that's not available to the family oriented, I've missed a lot, too. I've missed what it's like to have a kid. I've missed having someone that I'm intimately connected with tell me I'm their everything and they're mine. I've missed baby's first steps, saving for college, offering my child's hand in their own marriage. After a day at work, my couch doesn't look happy to see me when I walk in the door.

Every holiday, every birthday, every SUV is designed for the family I won't have. At work, they want me to cover holidays so the people with families can be home with them. At dinner, I'm the odd man out, since most people show up as couples.

With all that complaining, I've had some great relationships while single. My former church in San Marcos, California comes to mind.

I joined a church in San Marcos after starting recovery that was evangelical. Having started in a living room, it grew to a warehouse, and eventually purchased a storefront building to house a rapidly growing congregation. This San Marcos church focused on young families but had a mix of all ages. The dim lighting and loud rock worship made services fun. It was a startup culture; growing almost faster than its leaders could keep up with. I was 37 when I started attending, and I made friends quickly.

A couple of guys started a men's Bible study with me. We met at the church in a little annex building that served as a coffee house on Sundays – which gave it a very social feel. The atmosphere allowed us to practice outreach and evangelism. We had a mix of single, married, and divorced men who came. We had men from all walks of life and some who were unbelievers. The fact that we weren't in someone's house meant we could invite anyone – no matter how little we knew of them.

I couldn't have hoped for a more amazing group of random misfits! I loved every one of them. Years after moving away from San Marcos, I still received comments on my Facebook page from those guys reminiscing about our times together.

Phil was in one of those scooter-chairs. Jimmy drove a big, beautiful brand-new Hummer. One day we went to the airshow at the nearby Miramar Marine Corps Air Station. We worked to get that half-ton scooter up a makeshift ramp into the back of Jimmy's SUV. We scratched the interior up pretty well – but Jimmy didn't care. It must have been hilarious to watch us figure out how to make it fit! We had a great day together.

Todd lived with his family in a Toyota Camry when his wife got pregnant. Charlie decided that wouldn't do, so he took up a collection and got Todd a bankruptcy attorney along with the down payment and a couple of months' rent for an apartment.

All the guys chipped in, and Todd didn't have to give his baby to child protective services while moving his family of four under a roof.

Alfred's son Edgar was diagnosed with multiple sclerosis. The two were avid motorcycle riders and feared their rides would be cut short as it progressed. One of the guys decided to enter in the MS Bike Ride to raise money for a cure – and dedicated his ride to Alfred's son. The whole group signed the rider's bib and gave it to Edgar, along with a picture of the two riders together – Edgar on his motorcycle and the cyclist with his bike.

This group was a great place to grow, to serve, and to learn how to share intimacy in a non-romantic, non-sexual way. It was rewarding to be a part of it, and years later, I'm still in touch with some of those guys. I think that's what Yuan and Hill were thinking of when they envisioned a spiritual family and friendship.

As wonderful as that group was, I couldn't see it replacing the intimacy that exists in a committed relationship. Perhaps there are people whom it would work for as such – just not me?

I hope I've painted a decent picture for this choice. Now the decision is yours: Do you pursue a rich life of singleness, or would you determine to move away from celibacy and venture into a relationship? Perhaps a better look at how being gay is or isn't a sin would be appropriate before such a decision?

PUTTING THINGS IN PERSPECTIVE

LUST AND THE "BIG M"

How big of a deal is it to be gay, as a Christian? There's a spectrum of responses to that. On one end, there are people who think that even if you're not gay, but you think it's okay to be gay, you're not a Christian and therefore going to hell.[1] On the other end, there are people who believe that being gay is no different from being straight, in God's eyes, and that gays should have every privilege extended to anyone else in a church.

While we're working through our personal beliefs, many of us are daunted by the thought that "being this way" could mean an eternity of damnation and punishment. If you've been brought up in, or currently attend a church that teaches "all sin is sin," it's especially easy to believe you're in big trouble – and if you're like me, you've tried and tried to not "be this way," with no success. That's because there are beliefs that simply fantasizing about something that's sinful is sinful. It doesn't give us much to hide behind!

Working this out could take some time for you. While you do that, it's important to put your position in proper perspective. One approach I've found helpful is to identify the problems every church has with sin, compare those problems with our own, and see if we have an opportunity to evaluate how hard we should be on ourselves.

I'm reminded of a conversation with a couple of friends about health and nutrition.

When I hit the tender age of 37, three things changed in my life: I quit smoking, gained 20 pounds, and watched my blood pressure elevate to the pre-hypertensive range. I was baffled. As an avid bicyclist and former smoker, my health should have been improving rather than going in the other direction. My doctor explained, "Andy, you're battling age, heredity, and a life of beating up your body. Now take this pill."

The doctor explained the alternative to that pill was diet and exercise, and eventually that's what I did. It was a slow process where I replaced a less-healthy food item with a reasonable substitute. One such substitution was soda water for soda. At one or two sodas per day, that was a pound every 10-15 days. Slowly, over several years and with a gradual increase in my physical activity, I lost a total of 50 pounds off my peak from these minor changes. I didn't have to take my blood pressure pills anymore and found that I enjoyed the exercise.

My methods drew some criticism. Bananas and blueberries were said to be high in sugar. People would point that out to me as I ate them, and I would explain they replaced my morning pumpkin bread from Starbucks and tubs of Ben and Jerry's ice cream. So, each step might not have been perfect, but a step in the right direction, nonetheless.

If you think I'm bragging about losing 50 pounds, you're right! But there's a point to it. One night, drinking my sparkling water out of the recyclable, single-use plastic bottle, my friends Mel and Joe started in on me.

"Do you know that plastic is bad for you? Those bottles aren't healthy for you!"

These were two young, good-looking guys who I really liked. Their statements filled me with conflict because I wanted to impress them but didn't have a good alternative for my go-to drink of choice.

I explained to them how hard it had been to replace the sugar drinks I had been drinking with soda water, and I didn't know what I'd do without that as a placebo. I explained the bigger health issues soda water played a part in solving.

Mel and Joe didn't care; they didn't budge from their assertion. It was as if I was part of some evil self-destructive initiative to kill myself with microscopic plastic. Then I noticed what was happening while we were having the conversation…they were smoking cigarettes!

Of course, I pointed out this bit of hypocrisy to them. It had no impact. We moved on, although the conflict remained unresolved.

My takeaway was this: they may have been right. Their inability to live by similar healthy standards helped me put my habit into perspective. Nobody's perfect.

I've found we can go through a similar exercise with many of our churches. For one, the topic of sex has risen in importance in church over the years. If we're honest, we'd find that sex and sexuality are a defining component of the Christian church – especially in America.

How important was sexuality to Jesus? Would it surprise you to know that of all the things Jesus talked about, topics like adultery, fornication, and sexual immorality didn't even make it into the top ten? And to boot, Jesus never mentioned same-sex relations one way or another!

If we look at how certain sins are treated in our churches, we might be able to breathe a sigh of relief when it comes to our sexuality. In this chapter, we can look at two important examples.

LUST AND THE "BIG M"

Lust and sexuality hits a sensitive nerve among conservatives – at least the ones I know. The Christian sexual ethic is a defining element of the religion and its followers. The stance on homosexuality is but one element. Looking at how Christians approach other aspects of sexuality can help us with our own.

Part of the Christian sexual ethic is the idea that our thoughts are as meaningful as our actions. That idea comes from Jesus' Sermon on the Mount:

> You have heard that it was said, 'You shall not commit adultery.' But I tell you that anyone who looks at a woman lustfully has already committed adultery with her in his heart. (Matt. 5:27-28)

As a result, there has been quite a bit of work done in the church and organizations controlled by the church to hide from lust in society. We protest billboards and advertisements, movies, and television that show too much skin. Internet porn has rung our Christian anti-sin alarm bell as a trap that supposedly leads to addiction and horrible emotional damage to teenagers and adults who view it.

In my early church small groups, we would talk about "the big M" - masturbation. We all knew it was forbidden, yet we all did it. There's a long running joke about statistics showing that among men, "95% admit to masturbating and 5% lie." What do conservative Christian leaders have to say about it?

Protestants have been divided over the topic of masturbation, and it remains a discussion that occurs in the margins of our churches. Could you imagine what would happen if churches expelled everyone who regularly masturbated? Kept them from leadership positions?

The following is a compilation of published thoughts about masturbation from the conservative Christian community. They are listed with their sources on religioustolerance.org:

- Masturbation is a form of adultery
- Masturbation is sinful because of the sexual fantasies it generates
- Masturbation is a form of impurity and uncleanness
- Masturbation is addictive and a misuse of sexuality
- Masturbation is a violation of God's purpose for sex
- Masturbation is not part of God's plan
- Masturbation can lead to infidelity and other sinful and criminal behavior[2]

Does this list sound like it would line up with the views of churches you've frequented? Does it also sound like how conservative Protestants describe homosexuality? To find out, just replace "masturbation" on that list with "being gay," and see if any or all those statements are familiar to you.

Some Protestant leaders suggest Christians should masturbate without thinking of another person, or instead thinking of their generic "future spouse" when performing the act. I assume most of these people have masturbated and understand its definition. I don't know how they can realistically expect that suggestion to be followed. Does training oneself to vent sexual energy without visualizing our sexual partner as a person alleviate issues, or might it cause worse ones?[3]

I learned about this opposition to self-pleasure while I was a relatively new believer, and it left me dismayed, until I heard Dr. James Dobson weigh in on the topic. Dr. Dobson was the founder and leader of "Focus on the Family." This para-church ministry was one of the most influential political voices in conservative, Christian America. I listened to his radio broadcast regularly on our local Christian station.

One day, Dr. Dobson surprised me. I remember hearing on the radio that he had written a letter in response to a question regarding masturbation, and basically said your teen will be hurt worse by the guilt and shame from repeated failure than by the act itself. The message was to be reasonable and loving when it came to masturbation, and not make too big a deal out of it.

Here were some of Dr. Dobson's points:

"We can say without fear of contradiction that there is no scientific evidence to indicate that this act is harmful to the body."

"It is as close to being a universal behavior as is likely to occur."

"Boys and girls who labor under divine condemnation can gradually become convinced that even God couldn't love them."

"Attempting to suppress this act is one campaign that is destined to fail — so why wage it?"

"This kind of 'reasonable' faith taught to me by my parents is one of the primary reasons I never felt it necessary to rebel against parental authority or defy God."[4]

Dr. Dobson urged us to get real when addressing this act. But the question in my mind is, should the fact that everybody does it allow us to treat it differently than other sins? Second, what would happen if we applied this advice to the rest of our sexuality?

Today, Focus on the Family has removed Dr. Dobson's original letter, and re-characterized Jesus' definition of adultery: "God tells us in Matthew 5:28 that fantasy hurts a person's mental and spiritual purity."[5]

Why the shift in God's standard? Why flee from the word "adultery," which is clear in the text of Matthew 5:28? After all, the predominant Christian view is that fantasizing about someone who's not your spouse is adultery.

Could it be that even the most conservative believers acquiesce to a more reasonable standard when it becomes apparent that success is impossible?

One thing is certain: when everyone does it, the rules change. The hard-liners scatter, trying to find a way to live their sinful lives without acknowledging they're caught. All, except Dr. Dobson, who simply told us not to freak out about it.

As we approach our sexuality and recognize a standard that is so exacting it drives some to harm, perhaps we can lighten up on ourselves the same way Dr. Dobson recommended on this similar issue!

GOSSIP

It was Pride weekend in Long Beach, and a friend and I were eating at my favorite Mexican restaurant near all the festivities. As I looked down at my tacos, I felt the presence of someone standing next to me – standing over me was more like it. It was a giant nun. With a beard!

The Sisters of Perpetual Indulgence are kind of like an LGBTQ Rotary Club. They're known for their outlandish exaggerations with makeup and nun-drag. They make appearances at lots of events to either volunteer or fundraise for causes that impact the gay community.

This sister stood about six-foot four on top of some sort of black platform boots that added a couple of inches to their height. The giant nun had a wavy flowing habit and white makeup above the black accents around their beard and handlebar-waxed mustache. Long lashes fluttered as a deep, booming voice said, "Hi, Andy!"

I had no idea who this was, and the nun seemed to enjoy keeping me in suspense. Finally, they let me know – "It's Ned! How are you?"

Ned had been a member of the college group who came out while he was there. He and his boyfriend were regular attendees – during a time I would have taught homosexual behavior was a sin that should be avoided.

How was I, he asked? Scared – that a gay nun-man who knew me from church would see me within a mile of a pride celebration! I kept my fear to myself and asked, "So Ned, do your parents know about this latest hobby?"

"Well, my dad does, and he's worried about how my mom will react. But otherwise yeah, he's fine with it!"

I contacted Ned while writing this story. He told me what it was like to be a gay person in our college ministry. He felt the church leadership had been supportive of him and his attendance.

Not so for the whole group, however.

Ned told me how a few members of our group decided to out him to the rest of the congregation. In a congregation of more than 4,000 people that was more than a little uncomfortable. He did what a lot of self-respecting people would do in that situation – he left.

Ned was the victim of church gossip; it cost him a church community, and the church a good heart. Not one of the gossipers was admonished for their behavior.

Today, he remains a pleasant, successful man who makes a positive impact on the world. Less active in the Sisters, he now raises money regularly for the AIDS Lifecycle event – a bike ride from San Francisco to Los Angeles that benefits AIDS charities.

There are dozens of verses across the Bible dealing with the sin of gossip. It runs as a theme through just about every genre of biblical literature. Yet, it's almost a universal problem in congregations, regardless of their stance on the Bible and sin.

Imagine if each church that experienced gossip among its members and leaders reacted the same way as they did with issues of sexuality? Would there be anyone left to lead the church? Anyone in the congregation at all?

When a church treats what it perceives as your sin differently than other people whose sins it faces, it's a signal that it may be setting an unreasonable standard for you to meet. While you figure out what you're going to do with that information, you can at least relax a bit knowing you're not the problem!

A BIBICAL PERSPECTIVE

While there are six contested verses in the Bible that may be about homosexuality, did you know there are hundreds of verses that point out how we should treat the poor?

While roughly ten percent of our population is gay, twelve percent of people in the world don't have enough food to eat. Which condition should bother us more? Can we allow the frequency and clarity of Scripture on each topic to set our priorities?

We've got to put our issue in perspective. Not so our churches will stop treating us as infidels, but so we can look at ourselves in the mirror and know we're all right. We need to understand the worst-case for us is we're flawed, not condemned, in the same way that our brothers and sisters at church are flawed and not condemned. That, apart from whether being gay is a sin.

In fact, God paved the way for us with an infinitely valuable sacrifice for sin and fulfilling the Law so we could spend our days doing our parts in sharing God's love.

WHAT THE BIBLE SAYS

"BIBLE SAYS IT, I BELIEVE IT, THAT SETTLES IT!"

That's the club I'm in. I believe that a loving God would want us to know His story, and that He preserved the Message throughout the years, even millennia, so we could have a reliable testimony in how to have a relationship with Him. That's why I pay attention when the Bible makes statements about homosexuality – whether it be about acts, lifestyle, or identity.

As not-straight people, it's tough to read the passages that seem to mention the practice. The message we receive from a quick read in English:

- We are sodomites. (Gen 19:13)
- We are an abomination. (Lev. 18:22, 20:13)
- We've exchanged the truth for a lie, dishonored our bodies, worshipped and served the creature rather than the Creator, and have been given to vile passions. (Rom. 1:27)
- We will not inherit the Kingdom of God. (1 Cor 6:9)

- We are lawless, insubordinate, ungodly, and sinners;
  unholy and profane. (1 Tim 1:9-10)

That's a pretty depressing list at first glance; even worse at second, third, and fourth glance. In fact, researching this left me depressed every time I read the non-accepting position on homosexuality.

In recent years, a host of trained theologians have emerged who argue the Bible doesn't condemn homosexuality the way we practice it today. They're from a variety of backgrounds, but are increasingly evangelicals, who once held non-accepting views.

Is this a glimmer of hope we can cling to, that we might not be the horrible sinners we once thought?

MODERN DAY GALILEOS

There are contemporary books by Mel White, Matthew Vines, Justin Lee, Colby Martin, and others that claim to hold the Bible in the same high regard as other conservative Protestants. They conclude the Bible doesn't condemn homosexuality. Several others date back to the sixties and earlier by priests and ministers questioning the traditional position on the practice.

People affirming these non-traditional positions are often called "revisionists." They're accused of heresy, fired from pastoral positions, and generally distanced from their fellow conservative Protestants. To many, one's position on same-sex relations has become a defining element in the term "Christian."

I didn't want to be a revisionist. The term made it sound like I was dodging the truth. After all, how could we have gone this long after the New Testament was written with almost no one speaking up or speaking out about an alternative interpretation of these passages?

Considering this conundrum, I was fortuitously introduced to Copernicus, Galileo, and the abolitionist movement in the United States. I found that these revisionists, rather than dodging the truth, were attempting to uncover it.

In the 17th century, Galileo had the audacity to claim the Earth wasn't the center of the universe; that the sun and planets didn't revolve around us. "Geocentric" and "geostatic" were the two terms describing the biblical description of the universe. They meant the earth stood still, while all the planets and the sun revolved around it. Copernicus first posited a new heliocentric model with the sun as the center and the Earth in motion around it. Galileo later supported the view with his work. The Church declared the view theologically wrong. They charged Galileo with making claims that were in direct opposition to the Bible's teaching, as well as factually untrue.[1]

The Roman Catholic Church never formally renounced its declaration of Galileo's suspected heresy, and notable founders of the Protestant movement chimed in as well. Former Wheaton College history professor Mark Noll wrote, "For their part, both Martin Luther and John Calvin denounced Copernicus' heliocentric views as heretical (though a few other Protestants were early supporters of the new picture)."[2]

The church was wrong about this Biblical interpretation for nearly 1,700 years.

A bit closer to home was the fight to end slavery in America. The abolitionist movement remained largely a Bible-based debate. Pro-slavery advocates cited the following arguments:

1. Slavery was consistent with Old Testament direction from God in several places.
2. Jesus didn't condemn slavery.
3. Paul didn't condemn slavery, but instead gives instruction to both slaves and masters in its practice.

The pro-slavery conclusion to these points was to charge abolitionists with throwing out the Bible in making their argument against slavery. The disturbing part was the pro-slavery people had an arguably stronger biblical basis for their position![3]

Three examples in recent human history where both sides of a debate disagreed on what the Bible taught, in relation to the reality they lived. Two of the examples, heliocentrism and abolition, have been resolved. The third, a question of whether homosexuality is a permissible, acceptable Christian endeavor, is still debated.

With all the debate, we as Christians have a real need to get this right. We need a method to evaluate, or at least understand where these people are coming from, so we can make up our own minds and be comfortable with our choices. The answer to this need is a discipline called "hermeneutics."

HERMEN WHAT?

Hermeneutics is the art and science of literary interpretation. Hermes was the Greek messenger god, which is the root of the term. It's a science because there are rules to follow that can be substantiated experimentally. It's an art because knowing when and how to apply the rules takes skill and isn't always agreed on by all the scholars.

The goal of hermeneutics is to bridge the gap between God's mind and ours so we can apply it to our lives today. Five steps act as pillars to create the bridge between God's mind and our actions:

1. Inspiration/Revelation through the author
2. Transmission of the texts (copying and preserving)
3. Translation
4. Interpretation
5. Application[4]

The debate around the six passages in question for homosexuality focuses on translation and interpretation.

TRANSLATION

Translation is an issue many Christians have a hard time with. We read the Bible in our native language, which for me is English. The Bible, however, was originally written in Hebrew, Greek, and Aramaic. Although two of those three languages are still around, they've evolved significantly since the various books of the Bible were written.

Translation necessitates editorial decisions. If you speak more than one language, you're probably aware of that! Except for pig-Latin[5], no language translates word-for-word into another in a way that makes sense. The more readable the translation, the more editorial decision making is involved. The more literal, or word-for-word, the more difficult it is to read. So, what we get is a hybrid of sorts – Greek, Hebrew, and Aramaic words are translated with decisions made by the translators.

To see how this works, consider for a moment the New International Version's original translation of Hebrews 12:6:

> "because the Lord disciplines those he loves, and he punishes everyone he accepts as a son."

The word "punish" is problematic. When Dr. Henry Holloman, one of my theology professors at Biola University, brought this to the attention of our class, his question to us was, "Does God punish believers? Or was God's wrath toward believers exhausted on the cross?"

Many Christians would do theological summersaults to explain this passage in the "context of Scripture," when the answer is as simple as looking at the original word in its original language. The King James Version translates the same word "scourge."

The problem with using "scourge" is very few people today use it. In fact, I doubt many people would know what "scourge" means without looking it up. It simply means "to flog," which is a more accurate translation of the original Greek.

The important difference between "flog" and "punish" is motive. If I say I'm beating someone or something, I say so devoid of motive. However, if I say I'm punishing someone, I'm delivering a penalty for an action. It's retribution in that case – and that flies in the face of the Gospel of Grace.

Dr. Holloman had a witty way of calling attention to these important details in our understanding. Ignoring translation could bring us to some very wrong conclusions about God's will for us!

John was a good friend of mine. We were in a recovery program centered around growth in our relationships with God.

It required a good deal of honesty and action to look squarely in the face of our role in each conflict in our lives. It was scary, and because of that, easy to take a few days, weeks, or months off from the rigors of spiritual living. John had recovered from alcoholism, which was no small feat. One day I asked him how he was doing. John's reply was "moving at the speed of pain!"

Ever feel the pain that comes with living? Growing? Loving? What if you had the encouragement that your pain was causing you to grow – and it was a sign that the Loving Creator of the universe cared about you? It's the pain a loving parent allows us to feel so we can learn and grow. That's what Hebrews 12:6 says to us if we understand the original language. But if we read it at face value, in plain English, we walk away with the much different (and confusing) message of God punishing us for our sins!

Accepting scholars point to the original languages and translation when arguing against the traditional interpretation of a few of our anti-gay passages. Most notably are 1 Corinthians 6, 1 Timothy 1, and Leviticus 18 and 20.

The Greek word sometimes translated "homosexuals" in 1 Corinthians 6:9-10 and 1 Timothy 1:9-10 as "arsenokoitai." It's unique in its time; Paul may have made it up! The word is literally "male-bed." We, almost 2,000 years later, are left to translate it correctly.[6] Each side argues their position using the same standard for truth: what would a first century reader of this epistle (letter) take this word to mean?

A similar debate ensues over the word translated "abomination," found in Leviticus 18:22 and 20:13. The word "abomination" carries some heavy meanings with it.

Doing some work with a concordance, a person could find other uses of the word "toevah," which is the Hebrew word translated "abomination." In fact, the word "toevah" is used over 100 times in the Old Testament, sometimes referring to immoral acts, other times referring to ceremonial acts. It refers to several behaviors that are currently common in both Jewish and Christian households. In contrast with the word "homosexuals" in 1 Corinthians and 1 Timothy, the debate about this word centers around whether this is a timeless law of God, such as committing murder or stealing. Could it instead refer to a standard meant to set Israel apart from its neighbors, much the same way circumcision or dietary practices would?[7]

Here are a few of the other toevot (plural of toevah) in the Old Testament: Eating shellfish or pork, remarrying your first wife after her second spouse dies, and a Jewish man remarrying a non-Jewish woman. Equally abominable are a wife coming to the aid of her husband by punching his assailant in the testicles or keeping different sized measuring cups to defraud someone.[8]

So why aren't seafood restaurants protested by the same religious extremists who protest homosexuality? Why aren't there church-led weights and measures boards to determine who should be a member based on their kitchenware? Do Christian self-defense classes sin when teaching women to kick male assailants in their most sensitive parts?

Perhaps the word translated "abomination" has a subtly different meaning than what our modern English would let on?

INTERPRETATION

Once we've got our translation sorted out, we ask, "what does it mean?" That's the next step in bridging God's mind with our actions. It's also where a large amount of debate occurs between accepting and non-accepting scholars. We call this step "interpretation."

Henry Virkler describes the unique challenge of biblical interpretation in his book, *Hermeneutics*. Dr. Virkler sets up the problem in "The Naphtunkian's Dilemma" by asking the reader to imagine writing a letter to a friend, which got lost for 2,000 years. Three Naphtunkian poets attempt to determine its meaning. Virkler asks his reader to help the three interpret the letter by answering the following questions:

1. "Is it possible that your letter actually has more than one valid meaning? If your answer is 'Yes,' go to (b). If 'No,' go to (c).
2. If your letter can have a variety of meanings, is there any limit on the number of its valid meanings? If there is a limit, what criteria could you propose to differentiate between valid and invalid meanings?
3. If there is only one valid meaning of your letter, what criteria will you use to discern whether Tunky I, II, or III has the best interpretation?"[9]

If it were your letter, what probably ensues after asking and answering these questions is you meant something specific when you wrote it and finding a way to figure out what you meant is the best way to determine that meaning. That's what interpretation is all about.

A good system of interpretation starts with the meanings of words, phrases, and sentences, then considers the immediate context, then the larger context (where the passage fits into the overall argument or idea in the book). It then considers even broader context such as the type of literature, the author's personal perspective, the reader's perspective, culture, and geography. All these considerations bring us closer to understanding what the author meant.

CONTEXT

This idea of words that have ancient meanings within syntax, context, narrowing in on what the original author was thinking when writing the book from the Bible, is what we strive for when reading and interpreting Scripture. In this manner, we go through the process and end up with theology.

The opposite to that is called "proof texting." Proof texting occurs when a person starts with a belief then searches the Bible for verses that back it up. I've seen atheist pamphlets that claim, "the Bible itself says there is no god!" quoting Psalms 14:1. However, simply opening one's Bible to that verse reveals the full sentence:

"The fool says in his heart, 'there is no God.'"

Context extends from sentences and paragraphs, themes, and genres of literature. We should read the poetry of Psalms differently than the historical narrative that is Genesis. When we read letters Paul wrote, we should consider what was going on in Paul's life and the lives of the people he wrote to. We should also think about the culture, geography, and other influences such as politics and current events. We should seek to understand what the intended recipient of the writing would have understood it to mean.

Context is the argument Colby Martin appeals to in Romans 1. Martin holds that the comments on homosexuality "exposed the prejudices of the Jewish Christians and argued that their inflammatory and judgmental posture toward Gentiles was working against his very mission, and indeed was working against the foundation of the gospel."[10]

SCRIPTURE INTERPRETS SCRIPTURE

Another fun tool is to allow Scripture to interpret itself. That allows an inspired author, much closer to the source and writer, to give insight into the meaning of a passage. Pastor David Lose writes,

Ezekiel, for instance, refers to the sin of Sodom not in terms of sexual immorality but rather justice: 'This was the guilt of your sister Sodom: she and her daughters had pride, excess of food, and prosperous ease, but did not aid the poor and needy' (16:49).[11]

"Poor hospitality" when referring to Sodom and Gomorrah would be a finalist for the biggest understatement of all time, but that has been the Jewish understanding of Sodom. In fact, the interpretation of the sins of Sodom being related to homosexuality didn't surface until John Chrysostom, a 4th century bishop, attributed the story of Sodom not as an issue of hospitality but one of homosexuality.[12]

Pro-gay readers of the Bible hold that if we allow Scripture to interpret Scripture, we can correct the error of Chrysostom's revised view of that passage.

UNCLEAR GIVES WAY TO THE CLEAR

Each of the six verses have objections that call into question their clear meaning (at the very least). What do we do with a few unclear verses, with never-before used words, or ambiguity when trying to find out what these passages mean? In his book, *Protestant Biblical Interpretation*, Bernard Ramm says,

> In the concrete task of writing Christian theology this principle means that the theologian must basically rest his theology on those passages that are clear and not upon those that are obscure. Or to phrase it yet another way, 'Everything essential to salvation and Christian living is clearly revealed in Scripture.' Essential truth is not tucked away in some incidental remark in Scripture nor in some passage that remains ambiguous in its meaning even after being subjected to very thorough research. [13]

Applied to the discussion of homosexuality, if we throw out verses that are clearly talking about something different than two people of the same sex having a relationship, and allow Dr. Ramm's guidance to throw out the ambiguous passages, we may find ourselves with nothing to base a hard-and-fast condemnation against same-sex relationships.

Thinking back to my years of listening to Hank Hennegraf, the "Bible Answer Man" on Christian radio, I'm reminded of the guidance he would give on where we should divide and where we should agree to disagree, but not disfellowship. Hank would often remark, "the plain things are the main things, and the main things are the plain things."

Combining the two ideas from Ramm and Hennegraf, if we have an unclear passage, we needn't use it to tell people they're going to hell. We shouldn't use it to condemn ourselves, either.

CHOOSING YOUR PATH

It's daunting and discouraging to read and listen to people who don't agree with me. That remains true no matter what position I believe. It took me years to revisit these passages and develop my understanding of the Bible's treatment of homosexuality.

The reason it took so long was I had a deeper anchor that kept me in the Faith: God's grace, mercy, and love. I knew that no matter how badly I failed, I couldn't escape His love. Instead of focusing on my performance against God's divine Law, I spent a few years figuring out how to survive, and a few years figuring out how to grow. When it was time, I did some studying and found the various approaches to these scriptures refreshing.

For clarity, here's a table of the passages and the category of their objections:

Genesis 19:1	Context	Explained in Ezekiel 16:49, the passage is about hospitality.
Leviticus 18:22, 20:13	Translation, Context	"abomination" in Hebrew isn't the same as we know the word today - also the same section forbids things such as tattoos and
Romans 1:27	Context	This verse quotes contemporary literature, not Paul's view, and is used as a cynical hook in making a larger point.
1 Corinthians 6:9-10 1 Timothy 1:9-10	Translation	One word is unique to the letters ("male-bed") and another refers to sex with a catamite prostitute, or a young boy.

There's a reason this book doesn't have a chapter on each interpretation, determining who's right and why. Those books have been written – several times. I encourage you to read those books with this basis in mind. If the Bible is still a concern for you, I'd offer this chapter as a launching point to begin a deeper understanding of how to interpret and apply the Bible to your life.

You're welcome to take any position that makes sense to you. When considering these six verses, there are a few thoughts I hope you'll consider:

1. There are educated people who believe the Bible is God's Word and don't believe it teaches that same-sex relationships as we know them today are sinful.
2. Using the same principals of biblical interpretation as other conservative Protestants, we can call into serious question the conclusions that being gay is inherently wrong.
3. There are increasing numbers of educated, reasonable, believing Christians that believe the Bible doesn't teach that being gay is a sin.

For a lot of us, this will be reassuring – but perhaps not enough. After all, we're interpreting an old set of writings that are challenging to understand at best. So, what if we're wrong?

What if being gay is a sin? And if it is a sin, when and where does the sin start? In our minds with our attractions? Desires? Fantasies? Or does it start with a date, or a kiss?

Our next challenge is to look at how we handle sin, and how we understand the Gospel.

BEWARE THE BAIT AND SWITCH GOSPEL

Have you been told that God's salvation is a gift? I remember explaining that to the various church groups I taught. It's explicit in the New Testament. The Greek words "charis" and "charisma" used by Paul are best translated as "gift." The literal meaning of those words is "grace," which quite simply refers to unmerited favor.

Romans 6:23 is one of the well-known passages that use this word to describe our rescue from sin:

> "For the wages of sin is death, but the gift of God is eternal life in Christ Jesus our Lord."

That's how many of us came into God's presence and His church: an offer of free grace, an escape from the eternal consequence of sin, and a new hope. We were joined by others on the same journey, and we shared our experiences meeting Jesus in this way through testimonies, publicly sharing how we met Jesus. Our stories showed the people around us the deep and wonderful gift of salvation by God's grace.

As it turns out, mainstream Christianity believes a person is saved and will go to heaven through a gift from God – not something that is worked for or earned. Any person who holds a view that we work to get saved is branded a heretic; any movement that claims to be Christian and holds such a view would be considered a theological cult of Christianity. It is one of several central, core doctrines of the faith.

How many times have you heard (and repeated to yourself and others) that the major difference between Christianity and other world religions is our relationship with God is based on grace, rather than works? A gift from God through the person of Jesus Christ – the God-man who died for our sins and rose from the grave to give us hope?

This idea of our salvation being a gift can be a bit scandalous. It's difficult for us as people, especially in a this-for-that capitalist society, to embrace the idea of something for nothing. Everything in life, besides our relationship with God, is the result of an action we take or a status we hold.

THE BAIT AND SWITCH

If the Christian faith is distinguished from other religions by its foundation of grace instead of law, why is it that so many of us sit for hours listening to sermons that are simply to-do lists, focused on cleaning up our behavior? Why is there such a focus on whether we're in or out when it comes to heaven and God's kingdom? It seems like we signed up for a free gift, only to be hit with a bill to pay.

We could call that a bait and switch tactic. One website does a particularly good job of defining what a bait and switch is:

This offer is designed to lure you in, but instead of getting something too good to be true, you get a very different deal indeed (the 'switch'). It's either a much more inferior product or service, or you get what is advertised but at a much greater price. Either way, each instance is a clear case of fraud and is punishable by law.[1]

Here's what I mean when I say, "bait and switch gospel." The bait and switch Gospel starts with the message that God's grace is a gift, given freely. We accept it through faith. After we've accepted the gift, we're confronted with all the things we then must do. We either do the things to get the gift, or we do the things to keep the gift, or we look at all the things we must do for us to believe we have the gift. All three are examples of bait and switch. All three depend on our work, our efforts to be saved, even though we were originally offered a free gift.

The challenge we're faced with, works versus grace, hasn't been universally resolved among Christians in almost 2,000 years. Perhaps you've noticed the many ways theologians have attempted to figure out where our good works fit into God's plan of salvation: the reformed Calvinists, Arminians, etc., all have their takes on where our good works belong in the equation.

Rather than leaning on Christ's finished work on the cross and subsequent resurrection, I attempted to look at my changed life as evidence that God loved me. Thinking, "I used to do behavior X, but now I do behavior Y instead," allowed me to rest on my laurels instead of Christ's finished work on the cross. It led me to compare myself to the person sitting next to me and see how I measured up. It let me feel okay when I listened to sermons packed with the next set of behaviors I should get on top of. Surrounded by people doing the same thing, the difference between us and "the world" let me feel a bit superior. After all, even though I constantly failed, at least I was sorry for my sin and trying to do better! I had fallen prey to the bait and switch by thinking I was accepting a gift, when all the time trying to earn it.

I got saved by accepting a free gift. But at some point, John 3:16,

> "For God so loved the world, that he gave his only begotten Son, that whosoever believeth in him should not perish, but have everlasting life,"[2]

got turned into what I call "Johnny be Good 3:16":

> For God so tolerated the world, he sent his only begotten son, that whosoever behaveth as him shall have eternal life... maybe.

So just how do I understand the gift of my salvation? How do you understand yours? What does it depend on – our response? Our acceptance? Or is there something else at work that's out of our hands completely?

UNDERSTANDING THE GIFT

Shortly before Christmas in 2006 I met with my friend and mentor, Manny, to go through a discussion centered on things that made me angry.

Although he was a short guy, Manny's horseshoe mustache and receding hairline reminded me of Hulk Hogan. Manny grew up in Boston, giving him a classic Bostonian accent. He wore a black leather jacket everywhere and constantly smoked cigarettes. Underneath the hardened east-coast exterior was a wonderful man with a caring heart.

Our conversation was challenging – but got even more difficult when I tried to explain Christmas.

Christmas with my family had taken a rather bad turn for me. Every year got harder for me to tolerate the holiday. My sister lived in San Diego with her husband and four kids. My brother and I were single, and each of us, along with our parents had a two-hour drive to get to her house. That was much easier than trying to get my sister's four kids anywhere together – and San Diego was not a bad place to enjoy the holiday.

My sister, Susan, had never really nailed it when getting me gifts. I remember one time getting the soundtrack from a movie that I wasn't particularly fond of. I asked her, "what made you think I'd like this?"

She replied, "well, I knew you saw the movie, so I figured you'd like the soundtrack." I don't think I ever opened the package – and obviously, the fact I remember this 30 years later is telling of how little I appreciated her effort.

That Christmas in 2006, Susan didn't get me a bad gift. She didn't get me any gift at all. I had gotten her and her husband a pretty substantial gift card to a local resort. (Something their four kids would make almost impossible to use.) My brother got me an infrared thermometer that could measure the surface temperature of an object up to three feet away. (To this day I have only found one use for it.) I started to get irritated by how much I believed I put into getting gifts for everyone and how no one seemed to be returning the practice for me. Then my dad started in on me about how long I needed to stay that day when I had made some commitments later. I felt marginalized, unappreciated, and ignored. Feelings of frustration and anger overtook me.

Just two hours into Christmas, I couldn't take it anymore. I excused myself, with my sister begging me to stay so the kids could spend more time with me. There was no way I could manage it with the frustration I felt. I got in the car and made the two-hour trip home.

I explained this resentment to Manny, fully indignant and surely justified in my anger. An amused look crossed Manny's face. "Those weren't gifts you gave, Andy. They were obligations."

"Seriously, Manny? Christmas is for exchanging gifts. If I bring one for you, you should bring one for me. I get it if it's an unexpected guest, but this is family, and we planned it for months. I went over and above getting gifts for them, and they all got me crap or nothing."

"BS, Andy," Manny rapped the table with his fingers and glared at me. "A gift means nothing is expected in return; otherwise, it's not a gift. Besides that, Christmas isn't about you. It's about the kids. So, you need to grow up and stop being so selfish. When you go to Christmas, you shouldn't expect a single gift."

Did I mention Manny was Jewish? With a master's degree in a faith that has a gift as its foundation, how could I have strayed so far that someone of another faith could school me on something as basic as celebrating Christmas?

Two weeks later was Christmas. Manny gave me some direction in what I was to look for in the area of gifts. At that point, I was broken. Procrastination led to a couple last-minute gifts – but instead of buying my dad a gift card (Dad considered gift cards "cop out" gifts that didn't reflect much thought), Manny insisted I get him something he'd like. I got Dad a book on extreme golf courses (he loved golf). I found other things my family would enjoy and didn't go overboard with anything extravagant.

Christmas came. Everyone did exactly what they had done the year before that had driven me crazy. My dad jumped in to solve some problem my sister's husband wanted to fix, my sister forgot to get me a gift, and my brother got me something more ridiculous than before. Everything went exactly like it did the previous year.

It was wonderful.

Having zero expectations allowed my expectations to be greatly exceeded by whatever it was that I received that year. I couldn't tell you what I got each person (except the golf course book), or what they got me. I do know that I stayed for about fourteen hours and was relaxed enough to take a nap that afternoon. I finally knew (or relearned) what gifts were about. My dad and I worked together to assemble an outdoor trampoline. That trampoline survived the next 10 years in Susan's back yard, where it served as a reminder of this important lesson.

A true gift is a gift simply because it's given out of love and not obligation. It's received with no hidden agenda or strings attached.

Let's go back to the question from the beginning of this chapter. How is it we think God's gift of perfect forgiveness and eternal life is in jeopardy because of our behavior? Have we accepted a gift and then spent years trying to pay for it?

Perhaps the people who bait and switch us are wrong. After all, we don't need a relationship with works, we need a relationship with God. If we've accepted Jesus' work on the cross and believe He rose from the dead, we're saved. The fact there's confusion on what to do next is natural – but we don't need to get caught up in that in a way that keeps us from a relationship with God.

Lean on the fact that God loves you. Lean on the fact that you can't screw this up. Lean as hard as you can! The harder you lean, the more you can realize your relationship with God depends on the infinite love of an infinite, loving Creator, and the more you will enjoy your relationship with Him.

When I remind myself that I bring nothing to the table that dictates God's acceptance of me, it becomes easier for me to welcome someone whose sins are apparent into my community and serve alongside them as spiritual siblings. It helps me know that no matter what – sin or no sin, work or no work, I'm saved and going to heaven. Here's a quote from Josh McDowell's *More than a Carpenter*:

> And when Jesus said, 'It is finished,' the just, righteous nature
> of God was satisfied. You could say that at that point God was
> 'set free' to deal with humanity in love without having to
> destroy a sinful individual, because through Jesus' death on the
> cross, God's righteous nature was satisfied.[3]

When we think of how to deal with the challenges of our faith, let's set the foundation of our solution with God's gift to us; accept it and enjoy it as we move on to what comes, or should come, next.

THE GOSPEL FOR GAY PEOPLE

Jesus said,

> Very truly I tell you, whoever hears my word and believes him who sent me has eternal life and will not be judged but has crossed over from death to life. (John 5:24)

So...you heard God's word and believed Him. Are you sure you have eternal life? Isn't that the promise we received when we accepted the Gospel? But what about this sin of homosexuality?

You're a girl. And you kissed a girl. And you liked it. What could be worse?

You look at yourself in the mirror and see the wrong body.

You've deleted Grindr off your phone at least ten times, prayed for help, maybe even have gone to therapy. You're lonely, and the women you've dated took more energy than they've restored. The facades aren't working for you, and you're exhausted...

You may be one of the people who consider the above situations sinful. The people around you might. The point of the Gospel is to put sin in its place so we can walk forward in our lives, boldly, to serve God in a way that matters. Perhaps the pro-gay arguments many theologians make regarding the meaning of the six problematic, or "clobber passages," as Colby Martin calls them, don't hold water for you, you need a way to move forward that works.[1]

Even if you believe the pro-gay theologians, you probably still get attacked by doubts – otherwise you might not have decided to read this book. You need some reassurance that if you mess this up, you'll still be okay.

So, to my spiritual siblings, failed heterosexuals, and their friends: What could be worse than the abominable sin of homosexuality? And if I'm wrong, and this is a sin, how does it fit with my relationship with God?

The answer lies in how we approach the Gospel.

THE "DO YOUR BEST" GOSPEL

No matter how many times I read the arguments for and against the six verses that are used to condemn people like me, I still get a sinking feeling when I read the opposite viewpoint. What if I'm wrong, and all this gay stuff is a horrible sin that God hates?

Am I going to hell if I don't at least keep trying to be straight? Or abstain from all my gay behavior?

The question of whether a true believer would act on sexual

desires that are outside of God's loving plan for sex and love is extremely common these days. One message I've gotten from churches in the past is that we as Christians need to at least try to fight our sin. "After all," they say, "what good is grace if you don't respond by behaving better?"

My church friends would debate what it took to be saved in terms of our response to God's gift of salvation. There seemed to be a lot of Scripture describing good works and bad sins, and we couldn't all agree on how those fit in with the gift. Some of us believed you could walk away from your salvation if you kept sinning. Others believed you couldn't ever lose it, but the necessary result of salvation was a life of repentance and good works. A few believed to be saved, you needed to accept Jesus as lord of your life, not just as savior.

John MacArthur, a prominent evangelical radio preacher, seminary president, and pastor is notable for his position that salvation is not losable, but our assurance that we're saved can come from our behavior. He's most known for his position on Lordship Salvation.

Dr. MacArthur has said:

> So, you've got to be able to look at your life and if you ever are to know assurance, you must see a pattern of holy living in your life. You don't see that. There's no way that you can conclude that you're saved logically.[2]

How does that fit with the Bible? Ephesians 2:10 says, "For we are God's handiwork, created in Christ Jesus to do good works, which God prepared in advance for us to do."

Titus 3:8 says:

This is a trustworthy saying. And I want you to stress these things, so that those who have trusted in God may be careful to devote themselves to doing what is good. These things are excellent and profitable for everyone.

Each verse identifies good works as the result of God's grace – but what kinds of works? The absence of sin? An amazingly purified heart, or one that's progressively pure? If it's progressive, how do I know that it's progressed enough?

How many must I do before I can know that I'm saved? After all, lots of non-Christians feed the poor, heal the sick, and do many other wonderful things. How do I know the good works in my life come from God's salvific work in my heart and not just my own human power?

God told us we'd get His Helper, the Holy Spirit. He told us we'd enjoy the ability to perform good works, work in His Name, and be able to please Him through our faith. Did He give us an indication that we should use those good works to measure our salvation, sanctification, or faith?

Most Christians assume answers to those questions. Most of the answers are along the lines of reasonableness. Are you reasonably oriented toward God or away from God? Are you generally repentant? Are you sorry for your sin? Do you try your best? Do you try to try your best? These questions come to ease the pain of the stark reality that the model of holy living set up in the Bible is practically unreachable. People have dedicated their entire lives to getting there and most have acknowledged it's a journey, not a destination.

The challenge I would pose to you is, where does the standard of "do your best" come from? Which chapter and verse tells you the "reasonable attempt" approach to evaluating our practice of faith is the standard? I would suggest the Bible is silent on the "do your best" measure for our confidence in whether we're saved.

"Do your best" is also the Cub Scout motto – one I learned as a young boy. It worked great for my friends and me when we were in fourth grade. Today however, each time I think about the answer to how good I should be before I can truly know God's Holy Spirit is working in my life, I conclude "do your best" never satisfies the question.

THE NEED FOR PERFECTION

George Regas was the rector (senior pastor/ top priest) at All Saints Church in Pasadena, California, where I grew up. He used to say, "Wherever you are on your journey of faith, we welcome you to God's table," when it came to communion. He also said things like, "God loves and accepts you just as you are right now – no change necessary."

Those statements were like fingernails on a chalk board to me when I became an evangelical in my mid-twenties. "Of course God accepts you; the point is that you need to repent and change to grow in Christ's image," was what I thought. Grace alone just wasn't enough.

I got those ideas from fervent listening to Christian radio, attending church twice a week with a couple of Bible studies thrown in for good measure, and eventually getting into grad school. Then, while studying various answers to challenges Mormon missionaries would present to our beliefs, I found the Sermon on the Mount in Matthew's Gospel.

Jesus was drawing crowds. He had called a few disciples and was going around healing the sick and casting out demons.

People who were hopelessly cast out of society suddenly had lives returned to them. As the crowds gathered, Jesus taught them perhaps the most famous of his teachings, the Sermon on the Mount.

The Sermon on the Mount begins with the beatitudes. Here are a few of them:

> Blessed are the poor in spirit,
>> For theirs is the kingdom of heaven.
>> Blessed are those who mourn,
>> For they shall be comforted.
>> Blessed are the meek,
>> For they shall inherit the earth… (Matt. 5:3-5)

Does that make you feel as good as it makes me feel? When I read this, the scene in my head is the Jesus I met during Sunday school as a kid. I imagine nice green grass, Jesus in a clean white robe and neatly groomed beard, with colorful birds and butterflies above and pretty flowers scattered around the people sitting at Jesus' feet.

I think God wanted me and the crowds to feel this way at this point. It was the "you go, girl!" part of the sermon. It's easy for us to see ourselves as the poor in spirit, the mourners, the meek, and so on.

In verse 13, however, Jesus started to take a different tone:

> You are the salt of the earth; but if the salt loses its flavor, how shall it be seasoned? It is then good for nothing but to be thrown out and trampled underfoot by men.

Thrown out and trampled underfoot? Hey Jesus, isn't this a

bit harsh? Can we get those butterflies and chirping birds back please?

That verse, and the following verses, start to paint the picture of God's exacting standard. Just think of the Pharisees and scribes during that time – religious experts. They spent their entire lives being holy. They were experts in the Law and the prophets. They were the example of holiness for everyone. With that in mind, we read verse 20:

> For I say to you, that unless your righteousness exceeds the righteousness of the scribes and Pharisees, you will by no means enter the kingdom of heaven.

Yikes! Jesus is still talking – the same sermon. He's gone from puppies and rainbows to, "You're all doing it wrong," and progressed to, "to do it right, you have to be better than any of the people who you think are doing it the best."

Think about what it would be like to have someone say, "unless you can throw a football better than Tom Brady, you're not even getting into the stadium as a spectator."

After this list of requirements and admonitions, Jesus sums it up in verse 48:

> "Be perfect, therefore, as your heavenly Father is perfect."

If this were a musical score, it would be a crescendo, or an increase of volume and intensity, that leads to a very intense conclusion. My reaction is, "just how do you expect me to do this?" Or more realistically, "Jesus, this is impossible!"

For those of you thinking Jesus intended the suggestions in

His Sermon on the Mount to be something other than requirements, notice his statement in verse 18:

> For truly I tell you, until heaven and earth disappear, not the
> smallest letter, not the least stroke of a pen, will by any means
> disappear from the Law until everything is accomplished.

These commands overwhelm me. I imagine the crowds felt
the same way. You may feel the same way. Look at that moun-
tainous set of requirements and tell how me the Holy Spirit
helps people achieve it – any of it?

Jesus had several encounters with people where He told
them they didn't have what it takes to follow Him, sit with Him,
enter the kingdom of heaven with Him. While this sermon is
perhaps the best example of God's standard of perfection
explained, there were several other times Jesus pointed to it.

What's the solution to Jesus' challenge? How can my righteousness exceed that of the scribes and Pharisees? How can we
be perfect as God commands?

The writer of Hebrews helps us. Consider Hebrews
10:11-14,

> Day after day every priest stands and performs his religious
> duties; again and again he offers the same sacrifices, which can
> never take away sins. But when this priest had offered for all
> time one sacrifice for sins, he sat down at the right hand of
> God, and since that time he waits for his enemies to be made
> his footstool. For by one sacrifice he has made perfect forever
> those who are being made holy.

As a believer, I've been perfected, forever. Mic drop. Jesus is now seated, work complete. He has fulfilled the Law.

Some of us get seduced by theologies that tell us there are different *kinds* of laws, and we are only freed from certain ones when it comes to Jesus' work. Ceremonial laws, dietary laws, and moral laws certainly have their place in Old Testament life. Some would have us believe that moral law remains in place, while the latest fad lobster diet is exempt from the Old Testament decrees.

Our problem remains: under any part or category of the Law, we remain condemned. That's its job – to point us to the Savior!

We either have eternal life, forever, or we don't. We're either forgiven, or we're not. The Law is fulfilled, or we're still under it. This is where the bait and switch gospel fails; it creates the illusion that following God's Law is necessary in the equation of salvation. It's where the do-your-best gospel meets its match; doing your best doesn't get you to perfection. Only Jesus does.

Make no mistake: If we say we are *under* moral law, we're still condemned. It all goes back to the standard summarized in Matthew 5:48: Perfection.

The "if you sin, you're screwed" doctrine distracts me from growth and turns my focus inward in a way that doesn't help anyone. I could spend all my time and money trying to change my sexuality, stay celibate, find a way to live with myself as a tragically flawed, unlovable object not worthy of a relationship. In the end, who does that help? How does it benefit God's Kingdom?

My personal failure became the title of this book, but it's much worse than a simple lack of purity. The distraction to fix my inner-gay, stole my service from people who could have benefitted from it. Whether time, money, love, or expertise, when I withheld myself from a needy world in favor of unnecessarily fixing me, I did my spiritual siblings an injustice.

Accepting that Jesus has perfected us is the foundation we need to stand and build on.

WHY DID JESUS COME HERE, ANYWAY?

Do you think Jesus came to clarify the law, add to the law, or fulfill it? Is God's ultimate purpose and desire to see us reach a state of compliance with His moral code in our current state of existence? It's certainly reasonable that the all-powerful, all-knowing creator of the universe could enable us to do just that if this were about not sinning. Or is there some other purpose to God's extreme demonstration of Love?

Let's go back to Hebrews and see what that writer has for us next:

After the promise of perfection and encouragement for perseverance in Hebrews 10, we find the "faith hall of fame" in Hebrews 11. The writer of Hebrews lists several Old Testament heroes and examples of faith.

The Church of Behave has elevated these and others to an almost unreachable level of moral goodness as our examples. But, as seminary professor and author Preston Sprinkle remarked in an interview with Religion News Service,

> I think people generally read the Old Testament morally, combing its pages for moral examples to follow. We need to be like Abraham, live like Jacob, and be a leader like Moses, Joshua, or David. We should fight like Samson, flee like Joseph, and stand up for God like Esther.
>
> But most of the characters of the Old Testament are not

good examples to follow. Abraham was a liar, Jacob was a cheater, Moses was a tongue-tied murderer, Esther broke more commandments than she kept and never even mentioned God, and Samson was a self-centered, vengeful porn star enslaved to lust and bloodshed. So if we follow our Old Testament 'heroes' as Scripture presents them, we could end up in prison.[3]

In addition to the examples Dr. Sprinkle gives us, consider David: confirmed twice in Scripture as a "man after God's heart" (1 Sam 13:14, Acts 13:22). David was an adulterer and murderer with a failed cover-up attempt – and while there were temporal consequences for his sins, he remained a man after God's heart and was remembered as such.

We're encouraged to look at some terrible examples of behavior in Hebrews 11 – while the author points not to their performance, but to their faith. How often do we lose that perspective? Perhaps it comes from our disbelief that we could gain God's favor with nothing expected or required in return?

Consider these in addition to the lineage Matthew gives us for Jesus. Of course, Matthew's list isn't complete, he chose who to list purposefully. And, on the list are a prostitute, murderers, idolaters, and apostates.[4]

What purpose do you suppose these hooligans play on the genealogy? It was to underscore the idea that Jesus isn't here to fix our behavior; that in the end, God is looking for a relationship that doesn't depend on our performance.

RUNNING OUR RACE

Moving on to Hebrews 12:1, the author sets up a metaphor of our Christian lives as running a race:

Therefore, since we are surrounded by such a great cloud of witnesses, let us throw off everything that hinders and the sin that so easily entangles. And let us run with perseverance the race marked out for us,

First, think about everything that hinders us from running our race. Would it be our possessions? Our money? Athletes during that time would often run naked – so the idea of not having anything bog you down is clear.[5]

What things bog us down? Perhaps our preoccupation with looking good, our goals to fund our retirement, home improvement projects, the guilt and shame that stops us in our tracks and makes us want to hide rather than run the race…

I believe our preoccupation with our sexuality also bogs us down. It keeps us from doing the good God planned for us. It keeps us focused inward instead of outward.

Throw that all off. That's what we're encouraged to do. The author knows we can't *not* sin. They know we're hopelessly self-centered, prideful, greedy, lust-filled humans – they are too. We are offered the opportunity, through Jesus' work, to throw off our faults, our shortcomings, and run unencumbered. Jesus bought that for us.

Take a moment, close your eyes, and imagine the good that could come of your life if you weren't so distracted by what to do with your sexuality. Think of all that time, energy, and money you could pour into something that helps another human being. What would your Christian walk look like if you could fix your eyes on Jesus, and live your life in a way that reflects His love for others?

Kiss a girl, and don't let it stop you from sharing God's love with someone.

Look in the mirror and feel how you feel about your body – knowing God's fine with you; God loves you no matter who you see staring back. You can be a valued member of the family while you figure this out and grow through it.

Grindr, no Grindr, your dating life doesn't have to be forced. Recognize what's keeping you from being useful to God's children and take it with a grain of salt. You'll figure out how to make this work.

The words of the late Reverend Jerry Falwell during an interview with PBS give us encouragement:

I don't think you go to hell for being gay, or for being promiscuous heterosexually, or for stealing, or for committing adultery, or drug addiction. I think you go to hell for rejecting Jesus Christ as your personal lord and savior.

1 John 5:13 says, "I write these things to you who believe in the name of the Son of God so that you may know that you have eternal life."

You've been perfected, as your Father who is in heaven is perfect. Just like He promised. With this in mind, perhaps a look what others have done in response to this gift will help with your next steps!

COMING OUT

Striking fear into the hearts of many Christians, telling anyone about our "non-standard" attractions is seldom a welcome idea. For years, my queer friends would celebrate their ability to be open with their sexuality and relationships. The thought alone made me sweat.

Choosing who to tell and when, how to have the conversation, and what levels of detail to share are all important. I'm still scared to some degree when I tell people, and I live in a very accepting part of the world.

Up until the 1970s, most people never knew any gays or lesbians. It was easy to think of "the homosexual" as a big scary monster who wanted to convert their kids or spouses to their sick perversions. Gays were fired, disowned, and institutionalized for their sexualities.

Once people began coming out, it became harder to uphold the stereotype that gays were mentally ill, horrible people. Many people, upon finding out their loved one, coworker, or friend was gay realized that gay folk weren't as bad as they thought. In fact, coming out has been the single most effective tactic in the gay rights movement. It turns out that recognizing gays and lesbians as human beings changes how most people wish to relate to them.

That change shaped opportunities for gays to rise. Here are a few examples of people who would have been labeled mentally ill prior to the 70s: Tim Cook, an openly gay man, was appointed the CEO of Apple, the richest company in the world. Annise Parker, a lesbian, was the mayor of Houston. Pete Buttigieg, an openly gay man, was a viable candidate for president of the United States.

I see coming out having both positive and negative possibilities. It is certainly an important personal decision for each of us. While there are plenty of books and stories online about strategies for coming out, the question we must answer for ourselves is, "Why come out at all?"

In making this choice, it is helpful to look at how others have succeeded, and at what cost. Three examples come to mind: Alice's story, Paul's story, and my own coming out story.

INTEGRITY

I met Alice at church in San Francisco. She and her wife would sit across from me. Alice often shared about her experience in ministry at an evangelical church. I was curious how she ended up married to a woman, and if her faith changed in the process. We chatted one day, and I got to meet a woman with integrity.

Alice grew up in a family deeply rooted in the Foursquare Church. Her grandparents joined in the 1930s during a tent revival in their city. Alice told me:

If the doors of the church were unlocked, we were there. My parents were always leaders in the church. I was very involved, always in every youth group growing up. All I wanted to do was grow up to serve and honor God. At a pretty young age, I knew I wanted to be in full time ministry of some kind.

Alice dated a few guys during and after college.

There was no attraction for me with guys. What attracted me was being in a loving relationship with somebody, was holding hands with somebody, was knowing that somebody was thinking of me during the day. There was never any sexual element to it. Plus, I was a 'good girl'— and good girls didn't even think about sexuality or sex until they get married.

By the time Alice was in her thirties, she had graduated from Bible college and ran a large children's program with over 500 kids and 100 teachers in a mega-church. She was writing a Christian education book and travelled across the country leading workshops on Christian ministry for children. She was single and wanted to get married so she could have children, but that was the only desire she had from a relationship with a man.

On the outside I thought everything should be fine because I had this great life, but something just wasn't right. I really struggled with depression until I finally gave in and went to a therapist.

Alice drove 100 miles to her therapist to avoid being seen by her congregants. The therapist asked her one day, "Have you ever thought that you might be gay?"

I thought that was the funniest thing anyone had ever said. I laughed. I said, 'are you kidding me? Absolutely not! Not a chance!'

Alice pushed the question out of her mind as ridiculous. A couple of years went by, and her depression continued to worsen.

I was really at a point with this emptiness inside that I couldn't put a finger on. I'd be praying at night, kneeling beside my bed, praying 'God, either show me what's wrong so that I can fix it or take it from me.' Because my life was good, but I was miserable.

One night I went to bed with that prayer. I said, 'I need You to show me what's going on here because I am so miserable, and I don't want to live like this.'

I woke up the next morning and I sat up in bed and I said, 'I am a lesbian!'

It was out of the clear blue. It's not something I had been pondering since the therapist had said it a couple of years before. I hadn't thought about it again.

It was like relief and peace crashed in with horror and terror...It wasn't about sex, you know, it was just about identity. It was something I knew intrinsically. As soon as I said it to myself, I knew it was absolutely true, and there was peace in that. There was just no question.

At the same time, I'd been taught all my life that homosexuality was a sin, so now what am I going to do? I'm going to lose everybody I know, and nobody's gonna care about me. I'm gonna go to hell…

Alice prayed for God to make her straight. Then she started

cutting deals with God, promising she wouldn't act on her new-found identity. She struggled with what to do next.

> I typed in 'gay' and 'Christian' into whatever search engine we had back then. What I landed on was a gay porn site run by a man named Christian – clearly not what I was looking for!

Alice was ready to stay in the closet. She thought that was the best way to honor God. She bought several books on homosexuality to disprove the accepting point of view – to back up the beliefs she had held since childhood that it was a sin and "horrible." It was the mid-nineties, and Mel White had written *Stranger at the Gate: To Be Gay and Christian in America.*[1] From this book, Alice began to see that being gay and having a relationship with God weren't mutually exclusive.

Two weeks after her revelation, Alice had a business meeting with Nancy, who ran an orphanage and Christian adoption agency. The two emailed several times and were on their way to being friends.

Nancy surprised Alice when she said,

> I need to tell you something. It's very risky because nobody can know. I need to let you know that, that I'm... that I'm gay. And if that stands in the way of us being friends, I need to know now.

Alice didn't tell Nancy about her own recent struggles and realization. Instead, she replied,

> I'm not going to tell anybody. Thank you for trusting me. You're an amazing person. You're an incredible mom. I love you!

Alice described what happened to her after that meeting:

I went out to my car, and I bawled the whole way home. I drove
with the window down screaming, 'Where are you, God?'

I was feeling out of my mind. I went home and threw myself
on the floor of my bedroom and wept, crying out to God to
speak to me, but all I could hear was silence.

I had developed a relationship with Jesus my whole life. I'd
always seen Him when I was a kid. He was a real person to me.
He is still. As I was laying there on the floor sobbing, I kind of
stepped outside of myself. I saw myself lying on the floor and
Jesus was standing over me with his hand on my shoulder
saying, 'I haven't said anything because you haven't done
anything wrong.'

I got up from the floor thinking, you know what? I haven't
changed. I love Jesus! I love God as much as I ever have!

So, Alice came out. She started with her brother, Steve.

I adored Steve and I was sure I was going to lose him as my
brother. But Steve said, 'Sis, I don't get it, this whole gay thing.'
But then he said, 'I know who you are. I want you to be happy.
I'll always love you!'

Steve went with her when she came out to the senior pastor
of the mega-church where she worked. She had given notice a
few weeks earlier without giving a reason. Now she sat in front
of the pastor and his wife and explained why she had to leave,
and why she didn't feel comfortable preaching on her last
Sunday at the church, as was the tradition for departing clergy.
Her plan was to find a position on staff at an affirming church –

one that welcomed people of all sexualities. While the conversation seemed to go well, the next morning proved otherwise.

The pastor called Alice into his office and said, "I need to ask that for the next two weeks that you're at church, that you not be alone with any of the children, that you not accompany any of them to the restroom, that you not have them sit with you."

The pastor gave more "suggestions," sending a clear message to Alice that after 15 years of caring for thousands of children in the church, she was no longer seen as trustworthy to be with them as a gay woman.

Alice had mixed results coming out to the rest of the people in her life. A Christian educators association she had worked with for a number of years informed her she wouldn't be invited back as a speaker. Her publisher called and told her she'd need to submit her book under a pseudonym because the evangelical consumers wouldn't approve of her lifestyle.

Alice's response was, "well, if I'm an abomination, then surely what I've written is an abomination; so how could you use it?" With that, she walked away from the book deal.

She described friends who wouldn't answer the phone when she called. Other friends couldn't understand what she was doing.

All that was crushing, but even when all of that was happening, at no point did I say I wanted a 'do over;' to go back and not ever have come out. I felt bad that people were hurting, but that was their choice. I was just being who I knew I was. I did not take people's pain lightly. I did not take their confusion lightly, but never did I regret coming out.

In response to her difficulty finding a gay Christian website,

Alice started her own. First with a Geocities page (in the 90s, Geocities was a popular place to host and create personal web pages) that had her story of reconciling her faith and sexuality. Over the following years she expanded her website, which became a source of fellowship and support for thousands of women.

In the end, after realizing that she was gay, it was two weeks of internal struggle, and a couple of months before making the decision to come out. What was it that made this process so quick for her?

> I think part of it was if I knew anything my church had taught me all those years it was that God loved me.
>
> God loved me. They never gave qualifiers for that. There weren't 'ands' or 'buts.' When I was a little girl growing up in Sunday school, it was just 'God loves you. You are God's creation. God made you.'
>
> I think what made it so easy for me as compared to other people's journeys was, I didn't know anything else except that I knew that I was loved by God, and I knew with every fiber of my being I loved God in return. That's all that mattered.

When I think of Alice's story, I'm impressed by her ability to face and acknowledge hard truths about herself and respond in truth in her life. When I apply the definition of integrity, I often think of a thing that performs as promised. A thing that is as it appears or presents. A steel beam is rated at a certain strength – unless its integrity is compromised.

Alice ran her life such that what you see is what you get. Once aware of them, she didn't hide important parts of herself away. That, to me, is integrity.

SERVICE TO THE GOSPEL

Paul is my pastor. He's the rector of my church. We're Episcopal, but have no organ, no kneeling rail for communion, and no
altar separated from pews. We sit facing each other, sing a
cappella, dance during services, serve each other communion,
and choose our own saints to paint on the walls. Paul is a gay
man, married to a man named Grant, leading a church that's
about two-thirds straight people.

Standing 6'5", Paul looks a lot like Peyton Manning, with a
deep voice reminiscent of Alan Rickman. Paul knew he was gay
when he was five. He grew up in a conservative church in Houston. He described many of the people and organizations he met
as simply not having the vocabulary to speak to or about gays
and the Faith.

Paul became an evangelical, born-again believer through
InterVarsity Fellowship in college, and then attended Fuller
Seminary, the largest evangelical seminary in the world, for his
master's degree. At Fuller, Paul attempted sexual orientation
conversion therapy through an ex-gay organization called Desert
Stream Ministries. He thought Andrew Comiskey, the founder
of the ministry, might be able to cure him.

Desert Stream assigned a counselor to meet with Paul on
campus. Paul described his months of therapy as "dodgy,"
meeting at first in a room he thought was a repurposed broom
closet. Paul described his last encounter with his counselor:

> The last thing I remember him saying is, 'my wife is going to be
> out of town this weekend, and I know that I can spend the
> whole weekend apart from her and not just think about men.'

I thought, 'That's not me, because I can't spend a moment of my day not thinking about men.'

I broke up with Desert Stream. I didn't succeed.

I was a young, celibate, confused man living in Southern California in the eighties. The overlay to this was the AIDS crisis, which I remember hearing about for the first time when I was in college.

I was like, 'Oh, so you get sick and die from having sex.'

All I knew to do about that was to be frightened. It was a motivation for me not to try and have random sexual encounters with people, which was probably a good thing.

Paul graduated Fuller Seminary and returned to Houston, where he started work in an Episcopal cathedral.

In my early career, the church taught me how to lie well, which is not obviously what we're supposed to do. I was gay. Everybody knew I was gay. That's the funny thing about not being out of the closet; everybody knows you're gay.

The struggle was to be honest and loving and real with myself and with everybody else.

At a family dinner, Paul announced he was dating someone. His father, without looking up from the salad bowl he was eating from, retorted "Boy or girl?"

That's how I ultimately came out to my family. I told Dad I was dating Grant. 'He's a lawyer and he works in democratic politics,' which I think bothered my father more than the fact that I was gay.

I made a list of people I wanted to come out to; people who

were important to me at different phases of my life. I would engage these conversations with people and check them off in my journal. I remember the conversations very clearly. The common thread was, 'yeah, we know this.'

People were gentle about it or kind or funny about it. I don't think anybody was really scandalized.

Paul was offered a position with a church in San Francisco. It was an opportunity to leave what he considered a homophobic diocese, and he accepted it.

I asked Paul if there was anything he regretted about how or when he came out. Paul described an article in the *Houston Chronicle* – an article on the front page of the features section with a full color picture of Paul and Grant holding hands in front of their house. The article described Paul's decision to move to a diocese where it was easier to be a gay priest.

My whole adult life has been around the proclamation of the Gospel. Being closeted, you can't really proclaim the Gospel fully because you can't be fully yourself. The invitation of the gospel is to inhabit that story; to live into that story with your whole life and everything about you. Before I came out it was hard to know how to tell the truth about anything, including the Gospel.

When you're closeted and you're preaching, it doesn't diminish the power of the Gospel, but it diminishes the power of the proclamation, which is I think, one of the cruelest things for Christian leaders who are gay but closeted. I believe many of them are gifted and that the Holy Spirit has called them to this work and has given them the power to do it. Yet, they're unable to fully serve the Gospel because of the decisions they've made about being dishonest. That's a terrible waste. That's a terrible waste of the potential of the church to do greater good.

I used to be a part of the Wild Goose Festival, which is an art, music, and justice gathering in North Carolina. A couple thousand people get together in the summer for a weekend. I was on stage with a couple of other speakers. A member of the audience asked, 'what can the church do to help queer people?'

I said, 'The only thing the church can do that will make any difference is for the church to come out and say that we're gay, because we're all one body.'

Afterwards, a man came up to me and said,

'I just want to let you know that I really appreciate what you said about coming out. My son is 17. Last summer he came to me and said, "Today's the day that I was either going to kill myself or tell you that I'm gay. So, I want to tell you that I'm gay."'

I was crying. The father was crying. I said to him, 'You got such a gift! And now you have a responsibility to share that gift with everybody.'

What I mean to say is the church has got to come out and not deny that this is who we are and not try to change it into what it's not, which is about fear and all that other stuff. God made us the way we are.

God made us queer. And that's where the rejoicing is. The only thing that makes any difference is to be honest, to come out and tell our stories.

LOVE

Moving to San Francisco from San Diego, I kept my sexuality to myself at work but didn't guard it too much. Good thing, too. I remember walking through the infamous Folsom Street Fair, only to see one of my company's human resources staff running around in just a jock strap and tennis shoes. If I were trying to hide anything, just showing up to that event would have been a problem.

Up until my move, my sexuality was no one's business. The only time I would come out to someone was if being in the closet made me uncomfortable or feel like I was lying. A few roommates in San Diego fit that bill, so I let them know. Otherwise, I was a "normal straight guy." Except for all my gay friends. And a couple of apps on my phone.

I'll never forget coming out to my family. I started with my parents when I was 43.

My parents were in their 70s. Mom always reminded me of Angela Lansbury, and reinforced that conception with *Murder, She Wrote* being one of her all-time favorite TV shows. She was very accommodating – perfectly happy to sit through almost anything she didn't care for; seeing the rest of the family enjoy a play, ball game, or other entertainment was where she derived a lot of joy.

My dad is six feet tall and keeps his athletic build by riding his bicycle 100 miles or so every week. He golfs two or three times a week and, until recently, refused to use a golf cart whenever he could get away with it. He has a good-natured presence – a bit like a slender Tom Bosley as the dad in Happy Days.

My parents drove up from Los Angeles and arrived in time for a Friday dinner. The plan was to see San Francisco together on Saturday. On Sunday, we'd go to my church, which was about 30% LGBTQ, along with the openly gay priests. On the way, we'd pick up my gay friend Monty.

Monty was a flamboyant salesman of French descent. He

reminded me a bit of a dark-haired, bearded Patrick Swayze. It seemed like Monty and I led parallel lives; he was a drum major in high school, as was I. He too was a born-again Christian who ultimately left the church, unable to reconcile his sexuality with his beliefs. Like me, he recovered from addiction. We set out on a search for a church that ultimately led to St. Gregory of Nyssa in San Francisco and would regularly make the 20-mile drive together on Sundays.

So there I was, surrounded by gay friends and gay-friendly organizations, never having come out to my parents. It felt like lying.

After dinner on Friday, Mom announced, "Well, it's getting a bit late, and we'd like to go to bed."

Not so fast, Mom!

Mom, Dad, I want to tell you that I love you. And I know that you love me. I need to tell you that I'm not attracted to women. I'm gay – and I've known this for some time.

I want you to know the reason I haven't told you until now has nothing to do with you, or how I thought you'd react. I've always known you'd love and accept me for whoever I am. My problem was I didn't accept myself, and that's what kept me from being open and honest with you.

My parents didn't seem surprised, nor did they look upset. My dad said, "Twenty years ago, this would have gone over like a lead balloon. But heck, it's 2013!"

Following my parents, I called my sister and brother and had similar conversations. My sister told her kids and husband separately; my brother said, "what matters to me is that you're happy."

The next time I showed up for a family event, my niece Ella greeted me at the door, looked me in the eye, and said, "Uncle Andy, I love you!"

Coming out to my family was an act of love. It allowed me to express my love to others in my life and allowed them to love me. The more I did it, the more love I experienced; real love connected to the real me.

COMING OUT

Here's my proposal for coming out: Make it an act of personal integrity and love that serves the Gospel.

When you come out to someone, you're sharing an important part of yourself. You're allowing what's on your outside to accurately reflect what's going on inside. That's integrity, and in the absence of the threat of being roped and dragged down the street behind a pickup truck (this happened where I went to college), it's a virtue.

When you are brave enough to be honest about this part of yourself to someone, coming out can be an act of love. It sends a message that you're willing to be vulnerable and give them access to a part of you that most other people don't get. That's a special thing.

Finally, the idea that coming out is an important part of proclaiming the Gospel should play into our decision. If being a Christian is supposed to be contagious, how does our cowering in fear, self-loathing, and regret serve that?

You may find yourself in a place where you can do the most good by letting people know who you are.

SEX, RELATIONSHIPS, AND MARRIAGE

Browsing an LGBTQ Christian group on Facebook, I came across the question, "How did you find your Christian partners?"

The responses caught my attention:

Brandy said, "I have prayed to God for 21 years, 'Please God send a Christian into my life.' My answer? Nothing. Nada. Zip. zero. I wonder if God hears me?"

Rafael said, "Church."

David said, "It took 58 years but when I accepted myself for myself and was okay with the fact I might be single the rest of my life that's when I met my partner at an LGBTQ+ Christian retreat. We've been together for over 4 years. We are flourishing."

Ian said, "Ironically on Grindr!"

Chris said, "I asked God to send me a Christian and someone that would show me through his love for me that he was a believer. I asked God for a sign that the one he sent to me was from Him. God spoke to my heart."

Once we're walking a path toward a right relationship with God and with ourselves, we often turn toward questions around a romantic relationship. Everyone reading this book will have a different ideal of what that looks like.

Aside from those who choose to live in celibacy, we need to figure out what's right for us in the areas of dating, sex, love, and marriage. As Christians, many of us turn to the Bible to provide insight.

THE BIBLICAL MODEL FOR MARRIAGE

A master's degree in a theological discipline in hand, I was struck by the realization that I had no answer for how Old Testament polygamy morphed into New Testament monogamy. As a central issue to Western theology, certainly there must be a turning point or clear explanation – I just didn't get the memo?

I never found a biblical reference to explain the change between the Old and New Testament relationship models. I did find the line of thinking most Christians use to support their current view of marriage. There are two biblical arguments made for monogamous marriage between a man and woman. One is from Jesus' teaching, and one is from the creation model.

JESUS AFFIRMED STRAIGHT, MONOGAMOUS MARRIAGE

One of the arguments for the traditional Western view of marriage - one man, one woman, married 'til death do us part - is that Jesus seemed to affirm it in Matt. 19:3-6. The argument is that Jesus set the model that two will marry and become "one flesh," and He didn't say "more than two," or indicate that group marriages, or people other than a man and a woman could be married.

The problem with this argument is, when the same condition exists in other parts of the Bible, Christians don't come to the same conclusion. A clear example of this are the accounts of finding Jesus' empty tomb.

Two apparent discrepancies exist in accounts of the empty tomb. First, there is one angel mentioned in Matthew 28:5, but two mentioned in John 20:12. Second, the number of women who found the empty tomb is three in Mark's account, but two in Matthew's account, and one in John's account. Are these examples of books of the Bible contradicting each other?

Apologists such as Norman Geisler point out that just because an account mentions a particular number of people doesn't mean there weren't more.[1] So where there are three women at the tomb, it would also be true to say, "Mary was at the tomb." The only exception would be if the writer said, "Mary was alone at the tomb," or, "Only Mary saw the empty tomb." Since the text doesn't indicate the number was limited, we don't have a problem. The same would hold for the number of angels.

Let's apply that to Jesus affirming that a man should marry a woman. Would it preclude a man marrying a man? A woman marrying a woman? Could a man marry two women?

We don't know from this passage. It doesn't preclude God from setting that rule, but using a conservative toolbox to interpret Scripture, Matt. 19:3-6 leaves the door open for more than just one man and one woman.

If conservatives want to use Matthew 19 to establish the biblical model for marriage, they contradict themselves when attempting to defend the discrepancies between resurrection accounts.

ADAM AND EVE, NOT ADAM AND STEVE

Many argue that Adam and Eve formed the union that God would ordain forever. This is pared down to "Adam and Eve, not Adam and Steve."

There are a few problems with that. First, Adam and Eve's kids had to procreate with each other. So, the later laws against bedding your sibling would indicate a change in that perfect condition that God brought about. Also, it's not like Adam and Eve had as many options as we do today. With only two human beings in existence, non-procreation would mean the rapid extinction of the species.

A humorous thought came to me the other day. Sure, you could say Adam had one wife (if the concept of "wife" was even a thought then?). However, you could also say that at one time, Adam had slept with every woman on the planet! Using Adam and Eve as the model for marriage is problematic because it ignores their unique circumstances.

WHAT DOES A "BIBICAL" RELATIONSHIP LOOK LIKE?

Have you heard the adage "when all else fails, read the instruction manual," when referring to the Bible? Many Christians look at the Bible the same as they would instructions from Ikea on how to assemble a couch. If you get it wrong, the couch breaks and you're sitting on the floor.

The problem with this approach to the Bible is, no one told the writers they were writing an instruction book! To them, they were writing histories, letters, poetry, etc. I think if we read the Bible as an instruction manual, we set ourselves up for trouble.

With that in mind, let's explore what kinds of marriage were affirmed in the Bible. There are eight of them! We won't look at all eight, but we'll examine the most relevant.

The closest one to what we would call traditional today would be an arranged marriage between a man and a woman. There are a couple of examples of people getting married because of their love for each other, but most every other biblical example of marriage would appear in stark contrast to anything we see in Western culture today.

For example, a Levirate marriage was one that Jesus was challenged with in Luke 20:27-33. This type of marriage was mandated in Deuteronomy 25:5. When a man's brother died, he was required to marry his brother's widow. There was no provision to let a brother off the hook, even if he was already married.

Jesus' response in Luke 20 didn't condemn that form of marriage as not valid – even knowing the practice included brothers who were already married. From the silence, one could conclude Jesus didn't have a problem with Levirate marriage.

The closest God came to correcting any Old Testament character for the number of wives they had was King Solomon (wives + concubines = 1,000+). In this case the problem wasn't the number, but that many of them worshipped other gods. Their idolatry led Solomon away from the Lord.

Making things more confusing, the twelve tribes of Israel were born with Jacob as the father sleeping with four women – two wives and two slaves! If we are to say the Bible provides us guidance on what an ideal marriage ought to look like, wouldn't the original family for God's chosen people be a good place to start?[2]

The lack of a clear biblical model for marriage is what began shaping my current view of the Bible when it comes to setting rules for relationships. I began thinking that perhaps the purpose of the Bible was not to set specific rules around who to wed, how to wed them, etc. Instead, perhaps the Bible is written in the context of these relationships to demonstrate God's nature and character, and how we might apply values and principles within our relationships, however those relationships may be structured. In other words, the Bible may be describing these marriages without prescribing them.

Henry Virkler, in his book *Hermeneutics,* identifies the difference between prescriptive and descriptive language in the Bible:

> Descriptive passages relate what was said or what happened at a particular time without necessarily commenting on the veracity of the statement or the appropriateness of the action...Contextual analysis is the most valid way of differentiating descriptive from prescriptive passages.[3]

Rather than prescribing a formula for who can be in a relationship with whom, the Bible can teach us how to treat each other in relationships. In that case, the relationships we see in the Bible would be the examples used to illustrate broader concepts of love, trust, and respect rather than dictate what form those relationships must take.

HOW NOT TO FORNICATE

A lot of us want to get married. Along the way, we date to find that special someone. As Christians, we're well versed in rules that frame that process; rules that revolve around sexual touch. We've come to know sexual activity outside of marriage as "fornication." Looking at Paul's admonishment to avoid fornication, (translated "sexual immorality" in the NIV) from the Greek "porneia," may be helpful to us:

"The acts of the flesh are obvious: sexual immorality, impurity and debauchery." (Gal. 5:19)

Referring to our chapter on hermeneutics, we can remember it's important to interpret the Bible the way its original readers would have understood it. A leading translator and expert in ancient literature, Dr. Sarah Ruden says about fornication or sexual immorality in Galatians 5:19,

...porneia (from the word meaning 'buy'), which meant sex bought by the act and with no further obligation. A pornē, or prostitute, was normally a slave. Some had to parade naked in public places. Greek vase paintings show men beating them, evidently for fun. This was the institution behind Paul's word, and even when he isn't writing about sex for hire, he is probably emphasizing brutality...

For the polytheists, the essence of porneia was treating another human being as a thing. If I had been one of Paul's typical early readers, whatever else I understood from his use of the word, I would have picked up that treating another human being as a thing was no longer okay.[4]

Saying Galatians 5:19 limits sex to marriage misses the point. Paul wants us to stop hurting others for our entertainment (or for any other reason).

TREATING OUR LOVED ONES LIKE PEOPLE

When closeted people slip into fornication, it looks kind of ugly. It seems our news is constantly peppered with stories of politicians and other celebrities caught in the act, revealing anonymous encounters that split up families when they come to light.

There's the person in a heterosexual marriage who gets a little on the side with someone of the same sex. For some, that means an anonymous encounter under a bridge, in a public park, or at a hotel. For others it's a forbidden love that takes place sometimes for months or years without being acknowledged in their "real lives."

The result of this closeted activity, whether in public or otherwise, is deceit, exposing unknowing people to health risks, and participating in relationships that devalue or dehumanize the person they sleep with in secret. Dehumanizing one's partner occurs when they are used to meeting one's needs without concern for them or for one's other relationships. I've heard this practice referred to as treating a person as a sexual or emotional vending machine.

I encourage you to look at your actions. Lying, cheating, sneaking around, doing what could get you on a sex offender's registry, taking what's not yours to take, giving what's not yours to give. These are the kinds of things that put us in a spiritual abyss that we can ask God to save us from. They come from an underlying practice of treating people in our lives as things.

I've had experience with this on both sides. In my 20s, I was deathly afraid of sharing my name with the guys I slept with. I entertained men who treated me the same way. Then at some point, I stopped wanting to be someone's dirty little secret, and decided I wouldn't ask anyone to be mine. Making this change allowed me to look the rest of the world square in the eye. It changed who I saw staring back at me when I looked in the mirror in a good way. I'd encourage the same for you.

You may be left with a decision: Change how you're treating your secret or stop. And the fact you're reading this book means you may have tried to stop already.

I encourage you to develop a set of overarching values with which to treat the people in your life. I'd recommend you focus your energy on developing an ethic that allows you to be honest, avoids using and hurting people, and maintains your self-respect.

By honoring yourself and God's children, your sexuality can honor God.

CHOOSING A CHURCH

When I became a born-again Christian in my twenties, I swore off the Episcopal Church in Pasadena where I grew up. I remember going just one time after that – for my sister's wedding. Otherwise, I did everything I could to make sure my shadow never darkened their doorstep.

Why did I abhor my family's church? They accepted gays. They performed gay wedding ceremonies as early as the mid 1970s.

That wasn't all. They had, in my opinion, a loose view on the Bible as God's Word. They ordained women. They allowed people of other faiths to speak to them. And they were Democrats. For those reasons, I didn't consider them a Christian church – and that fit with my perception of the views of the conservative church I attended across the freeway.

When I moved away from Pasadena in 2004, it was easy to skip church – I couldn't attend a church that would accept the truth about me, and I couldn't be a participating member of a church that met my high biblical standards because I didn't meet my high biblical standards.

A few years went by, and I finally ventured back into a store-front evangelical church. I kept my sexuality to myself. Even as a 40-year-old man with no girlfriend, never married, no one gave me any grief or even asked a question about why. But I was leaving part of me at home every time I went.

So, moving to the San Francisco Bay Area, I again didn't jump into a church.

What got me back into the Episcopal Church was a service a friend recommended. He said the choir at Grace Cathedral in San Francisco was amazing and I just had to go listen.

The service connected with me in a way that surprised me. I remembered the symbolism for many of the little details in the liturgy and communion, and it resonated. Excited, I decided to join that church and called my friend Mike to share the news.

Mike was the priest at an Episcopal church near Pasadena. Mike and I had served together on a volunteer fire department, and he was our chaplain in addition to being a fire captain. I had known his family for decades.

Mike was happy about my decision but said he wouldn't allow me to join Grace Cathedral until I had visited two others: St. Mark's in Berkeley, and St. Gregory's in San Francisco. He explained that St. Mark's would be a more intellectual crowd and joked that St. Gregory's would be "whacky, but without too many heresies."

My friend Monty (who I described in the Coming Out chapter) and I visited St. Gregory's on a crisp, sunny November morning. As I walked up the steps to the whimsical building, a man whose beard made me think of Santa Claus handed us songbooks and fliers with the day's announcements.

The entrance gave way to a rotunda beneath a byzantine style mosaic with Moses, St. Gregory of Nyssa, Mary, and Jesus with the words "All that is prays to you." The upper walls in the rotunda were lined with rows of full icons called the "dancing saints," the focal point being Jesus in the center.

The church had chosen their own saints to include on the walls and had booklets to explain their decisions. The booklet explained why they had chosen Ella Fitzgerald, for example, "who overcame a tortured childhood, including desperate poverty and time as a prostitute, to become a singer of enormous grace and joy." Other notables were Queen Elizabeth, Lady Godiva, and Bishop Desmond Tutu.

The middle of the rotunda contained the communion table with an inscription in Greek I later learned translated, "He eats with tax collectors and sinners," in reference to Mark 2:16. The exterior doors opposite the entrance opened to a fountain for baptisms. To the right was the church's seating area, with rows of chairs facing each other on either side of a stepped-up platform.

Shortly after entering, we were greeted by a church member volunteering at the guest table. They encouraged us to print our names in red on typical rectangular stickers. The red writing let everyone know it was our first time at the church – which made us a target. An important duty of church members was to welcome guests – and they performed those duties energetically.

The service started in the rotunda where we entered. The ministers greeted everyone with a handshake and a welcome as the choir sang a capella. We walked into the seating area –to later return to the rotunda for communion in several lines, singing while we walked in step.

This was the weirdest church I'd ever experienced. I liked it!

After the main service, the minister sat at the front of the room in a small circle of chairs for "fifteen good minutes." It

was a time to ask questions, discuss the sermon, or just connect
with the church leadership.

I tried to get to "fifteen good minutes," but I never made it.
There was 100 feet between me and the seating area where
those minutes happened. To traverse those 100 feet, there were
as many church members welcoming me and wanting to engage
with me to talk about where I was from and what brought me
there.

I had been love bombed! I knew from that alone this was the
church I wanted to belong to.

The theological focus of St. Gregory's is Jesus, and Paul, the
rector, is biblically centered in his sermons. The people at the
church are passionate about helping less fortunate folks, and
many have ministries out in "the City" (what we call San Francisco in these parts).

On my way home, I called Mike, and told him I had found
my church. His reply to me was, "no, Andy, you haven't gone to
St. Marks in Berkeley yet – so you can't make that decision."

Mike was right: I was still one visit short. I spent the
following Sunday at St. Marks and returned to St. Gregory's
knowing I had found a home.

FINDING THE RIGHT CHURCH FOR YOU

What made me choose St. Gregory's? Ultimately, the style of
the service, while unique, didn't sway me. I enjoyed the services
at the other two. What got me was the focus of the congregation
on Jesus, the importance of serving their community, and the
friends I made so quickly.

My church is different from the church you will probably
choose. I imagine you'll choose a church that's more a style that

you're used to. The question we all must answer is, how do we balance style and substance? What's important as we look for a place to worship?

There are four factors to consider as you figure out what to do with your church membership. They include how you can serve, theology, community, and style.

Why would I put theology second? For two reasons. First, the church that won't let you serve in a capacity that fits you is not going to be a church you should be a member of, anyway. At that point, who cares what they believe?

Also, theology must be divided into two parts: essential and non-essential. I like to pare it down to the nature of God, the nature of humankind, and the basis of our relationship.

Some churches deny the Trinity (the belief that God exists eternally in three persons and one nature), which would change the definition of who and what God is. This would be an essential belief.

Some churches believe that baptism must be by full immersion. I've heard the saying, "If it didn't go in, there's still some sin!" to describe the need for a full dunk in a pool versus a sprinkle of water on one's forehead. This would be a non-essential belief (I hope), as our salvation depends on our faith in Jesus, not on how wet we get during a ceremony.

There are hundreds of Christian denominations in the United States alone, tens of thousands of Protestant denominations around the world. (I've seen some estimates of 40,000 Protestant denominations.) They are the result, mostly, of splits in areas of minor doctrines such as the baptism example, above. I'm sure, knowing how churches go, there are splits over more trivial matters as well.

To find your "perfect church," you need to figure out what

you can live with and what your deal-breakers are. You may absolutely need a hard-rock praise band with raised hands in a dark warehouse-like room to really connect during worship. When you find that church, you may also find communion either doesn't exist, or it's played down to a level that bothers you. Where your priorities lie will help you compromise in the areas that work best for you.

This brings us to making a distinction between substance and style. I'd encourage you to determine what elements of style you can sacrifice for the right community life in a church.

This all assumes we need to go to church at all. And, once we're there, what's our role supposed to be?

WHY GO TO CHURCH?

There are two good reasons to go to church: your parents told you to, and perhaps more importantly, to grow spiritually. Of course, there are a bunch of other reasons: you have friends there, a sense of belonging, it's a good place for kids, you get a sense of stability and tradition that comforts.

While there can be good music and great preaching, if your needs in church can be met by an amazing praise band and a fantastic sermon, you won't need to worry about whether the church accepts you as a gay person. If that's the case, you can sit in the back row and enjoy the program.

Something makes church more than just a show: Think about why you want to go to church – or why you should want to go.

YOU ARE THE CHURCH

There's a difference between going to church and being the church. Pastors are quick to point this out. We don't need a building to have a church. This is evident as there is no New Testament reference to a church as a physical building. On the contrary, this church "building" is built with you and me. Consider 1 Peter 2:4-5,

> As you come to him, the living Stone—rejected by humans but chosen by God and precious to him—you also, like living stones, are being built into a spiritual house to be a holy priesthood, offering spiritual sacrifices acceptable to God through Jesus Christ.

Peter goes on to describe Christ as the living cornerstone. Earl Radmacher, former president of Western Theological Seminary, writes:

> Even as Christ is spoken of as a stone, reared and precious, so the believer partakes of his character. He is a worked stone – a prepared stone – for which a special place is made in the spiritual house. Every believer has his niche to fill.[1]

If the church were a building, we would be the stones forming its walls. This metaphor breaks down because stones can just sit in the wall to do their job. Another set of passages help us understand the role we are called to fill in the church. These passages are about spiritual gifts.

WHO DO YOU THINK YOU ARE? GOD'S GIFT TO THE CHURCH?

There are a group of churches we refer to as "charismatic." Now, charisma generally means attractive in some ways, but that's not what the charismatic movement refers to. Charismatic churches emphasize the use of spiritual gifts – specifically those of signs and wonders, emphasizing the role of the Holy Spirit in our prayer lives and in worship. The word charismatic comes from the Greek "charis," which means "grace."

You've probably heard the term "spiritual gifts." Many associate them with speaking in tongues, prophesying, healing, and other miracles, although they encompass much more. There are three commonly accepted lists in the New Testament, along with examples of miracles in other places; Romans 12, 1 Corinthians 12, and Ephesians 4.

1 Peter 4:10 says, "Each of you should use whatever gift you have received to serve others, as faithful stewards of God's grace in its various forms."

About this passage, Dr. Radmacher says,

> God's Word explicitly states that every member of the body of Christ is gifted for service...and that every member is to be using the gift or gifts God has bestowed...The implication for the local church is quite apparent. There ought to be no idle members, but rather opportunities for service for every person.[2]

Our spiritual gifts are God's grace; they are for the church, not for ourselves. Rather than being blessed with a gift from God to you, you bless the church with the gift God gave you.

You are God's gift to the church!

How can we be that gift if we're not allowed to serve? The ability to serve is paramount to our choosing a church. It's also important to our spiritual practice as Christians. Without a church to serve within, we can't fulfill the role God has for us as believers.

WHAT'S IMPORTANT

This brings us to a couple of important take-aways. First, we need to understand that it's important to our growth to be part of a church. Second, we need to place the right priorities first when we're looking for that church.

Earlier, I recommended putting style behind substance, and all of that behind the ability to serve in a way that's appropriate to God's calling for us. While most of us can mop floors, some of us are called to other roles. If mopping is the only acceptable service for an LGBTQ Christian in a particular church, it won't be a good place for most of us to grow and serve. So why not find a church where we can?

There are trade-offs when we evaluate churches. For me at St. Gregory's, I had to get used to gender inclusive language used to describe God. In other words, God is sometimes referred to as "she." While I didn't have a theological position on God's gender, it made me uncomfortable for some time. Later, I learned there are biblical reasons for the pronoun shifts – things like God being described as having mothering traits and having a womb. Those answers came six years after I joined the church, so in the meantime I just put up with it.

We can get hung up on style of worship, style of dress, style of communion, even which Bible translation is used. We have an opportunity to put these distractions aside in favor of an opportunity to grow in a community that will allow and encourage us to find our calling.

HIERARCHY OF ACCEPTANCE

It's important to recognize some terms used to describe how churches accept LGBTQ people. Churches that accept LGBTQ parishioners sometimes use terms like "accepting," or "affirming," or "welcoming," to define their position on gays in their ministries. Because there's no rule or formal definition, it's important to ask questions about what a church means when it makes a statement about its acceptance of openly LGBTQ people.

Anthony Venn-Brown worked as an evangelical pastor in Australia who spent his career in church building projects and mega-churches. After coming out as a gay man, he wrote, *A Life of Unlearning: Coming Out of the Church, One Man's Struggle*. In his book, Venn-Brown identifies key differences between anti-gay (or non-accepting), welcoming, accepting, and affirming churches. In essence, the differences lie in the level of participation in the church, with welcoming meaning you can attend but that's about it, accepting meaning you can be a member but not much more, and affirming meaning you could be the pastor if that was your calling.[3]

Reverend Jeff Harris runs a church in Baltimore Maryland. He's openly gay but won't describe his church as a "gay church." Just "a church."

Reverend Harris spoke with me about the history of African Methodist churches in America and how it related to the progress of LGBTQ acceptance today:

Most churches in the era of slavery were predominantly white, and Blacks were not allowed to come inside. At some point they were allowed to sit outside the church, and they would open the doors. Then they let them in the church, but they had to sit up on the balcony.

About that time, a slave, [Richard Allen], was allowed to be a pastor. That opened up a door for other Blacks to come into the church and be 'kinda sorta' active, but not really active.

He gathered enough people to break away from the Methodist church, and that's how we got the African Methodist Episcopal [AME] church, which is a fully embracing body of Christianity for Methodist African Americans where they can all come. It was a safe space where I could be. My blackness, my Afrocentric-ness could be on full display in that church.

It was like it is today with gay people: you can come to the church, you can be in the choir, you may be able to usher, but you can't be in ministry. You can't be up on the pulpit.

We got the gay church because we needed a safe space to have all our queerness and lesbianism on display; their trans journey will all be on display and be fully welcomed and embraced.[4]

Reverend Harris writes about his journey in his book *Called, Claimed, and Commissioned: Shared Lessons in Accepting & Respecting the Spiritual Calling*.[5]

I've heard several describe the choice they make over their sexuality in the same way they make a choice about the color of their hair or eyes. With that in mind, what kind of organization would separate people who had so little choice in this aspect of their life?

Would you stay in a church that makes you sit in the balcony as an onlooker, or take a drive down the street to one that will allow you to participate fully?

THE PRICE OF INCLUSION

Stan Mitchell is a pastor at Everybody Church after having founded GracePointe Church in Nashville in 2003. He's straight and has led his church to fully accept LGBTQ people into the congregation in 2013.

I asked Stan how he approaches the topic of LGBTQ people joining inclusive churches. He told me he's seen two reasons LGBTQ people stay in non-accepting churches. First, some find it easy to continue rejecting the idea that it's okay to be gay, and therefore staying in a non-accepting environment is, as Stan puts it, "an insurance policy."

The second reason Pastor Mitchell sees gays staying in non-accepting churches is the relationships: friends and loved ones who are in those churches with them are hard to leave behind, even if they see themselves as mistreated.

Stan told me about why he feels it's important for gay people to find affirming churches.

I heard Rosa Parks in person a few years before she died. And someone asked her why she didn't go along that particular day. Why she didn't just give up her seat?

She looked at the young psychiatrist who was moderating the panel and said, 'I was tired,' and the whole place paused. And she said, 'but it wasn't a weariness of hips, and knees and ankles; it was a weariness of soul.

My entire life, I lived in the Jim Crow south with

grandparents and great-grandparents who still had memories of the slave fields. And what we had was better than those days. I was taught to straighten my hair, act as white as I could, keep my head down, don't look anybody in the eye and don't make waves.

They told me the worst thing that could happen to me if I didn't do that, I would end up in the county jail. All my life as a little girl, that county jail got bigger and bigger and bigger until I just intuitively understood that was the worst thing that could happen.

But one morning I woke up and I realized for fear of that jail, I had put myself in prison. I put my feet on the floor that day, and I said to myself, I will no longer be a co-conspirator in my own diminishment.'

For LGBTQ people who stay in non-affirming places, I think the only way they can credibly be in a place that conspires against them is if they're staying there out of their own strength and their own intention to put a face on this issue; to help that church change. I can't question that motive. I wouldn't ask anybody to do that. And I wouldn't judge anybody for doing that.

I was a pastor in a community where I moved the church from non-inclusive to inclusive. We lost 2000 members. We lost an $8 million campus; our budget went from two million down to $300,000. I had to let all my friends go. I went through a divorce; my wife was one of the ones that sided against us being affirming. It cost me almost everything.

I watched gay people in the community continue to go to non-affirming churches. If they were staying at non-affirming places because they were truly willing to sacrifice to see change, that's one thing. If they were staying out of convenience, then they are co-conspirators in their own diminishment, and that's wrong.[6]

Most of us won't have the opportunity to change the theology of a church. It's been tried and has resulted in splitting into 40,000 Protestant denominations! That's not to say getting a church to change is impossible, but it's helpful to know the track record of that endeavor.

The key is to get yourself into a place where God can use you and a place where you can grow toward the potential God has for you. You needn't bother yourself that one church won't accept you if there's a perfectly good church that will a few blocks - or even miles - away.

To deny yourself a place that accepts your service, you deny the church one of God's gifts.

HOW TO GROW

HAND IN HAND WITH GOD

"How was the retreat, Andy? Are you walking hand in hand with God?"

A friend asked me this on our way into a men's meeting. We had just returned from a 12-step based men's retreat that focused on our relationships with God. I was new to the group, and new to their lifestyle, which demanded dependance on God for survival, one day at a time.

I didn't answer. I had no idea what it meant to walk hand in hand with God, and that frustrated me. After all, I had a master's degree in a theological discipline, I had led plenty of people to Jesus, and I had taught dozens of church groups and congregations. Yet, the concept of walking hand in hand with God mystified me. Perhaps my frustration was the result of my focus on obeying God, being shaped by God, and working to be an acceptable sacrifice to God, while never thinking of what it meant to partner in service with God.

In the economy of a relationship whose currency is obedience, it makes sense to figure the best way to obtain that obedience so we can have the best relationship possible. That leads us to measure our growth in terms of how obedient we are to the thousands of instructions we find in the Bible, rather than our willingness, capacity, and availability to serve God's people.

There seems to be a conflict between passages like John 14:15, "If you love me, keep my commands," and Matthew 22:36-39, where the disciples ask Jesus to explain:

> Teacher, which is the greatest commandment in the Law?
>
> Jesus replied: 'Love the Lord your God with all your heart and with all your soul and with all your mind.' This is the first and greatest commandment. And the second is like it: 'Love your neighbor as yourself.' All the Law and the Prophets hang on these two commandments.

Is there an alternative to looking at Christian growth and holiness as simply the function of how little or much we sin? Shouldn't we measure our relationships with God differently?

Early in this book, I mentioned leaving the Church of Behave and joining the Church of Grow. The idea was about finding a church that could help me grow into the person God created me to be. That happened for me when I stopped obsessing over sin and started seeking opportunities to serve.

GROWTH THROUGH ACTION

When it comes to goodness, I've found my heart isn't always in it. So, if I follow my heart, I'm prone to failure. Jesus agrees when he says, "For out of the heart come evil thoughts—

murder, adultery, sexual immorality, theft, false testimony, slander." (Matt. 15:19)

If I rely on my heart to take me to the right place, I might be disappointed!

The men's group from the retreat I attended maintained, "where your feet go, your heart will follow." I've found that a very practical truth. When my heart's not in something, my feet can take me to the right place without having to feel it first. Please take this advice at the level it's intended – many have applied this to changing their sexuality and have suffered for it! I learned this as a teen working at a summer camp. The camp was in an island paradise – a cove and canyon on Catalina Island near Los Angeles. People would spend hundreds of thousands of dollars to buy yachts so they could spend a couple of weekends each year in our cove, and I was being paid, housed, and fed to be there all summer, teaching kids how to do things I loved – swimming, sailing, canoeing, and camping.

Every morning the staff would roll out of bed and show up for the flag ceremony at 7:15 am sharp. Even in such a wonderful place, I can count on one hand the number of times I was excited to rise and shine!

During the flag ceremony, I would zone out and try not to fall back asleep while standing in line. After the flag ceremony we would lead the camp in a song. Our songs at morning flags were always cheerful, loud, and funny, coupled with wild calisthenic gyrations.

Without fail, those songs energized me and made me cheerful – enthusiastic to work in paradise. Painting a smile on my face tricked me into thinking I had something to be happy about. Jumping up and down made me energetic. Pretending to be enthusiastic gave me enthusiasm.

So it is, I've found, with our relationship with God and with each other. I can pray for God to give me the heart of a servant, and there's nothing wrong with that. But couple that with doing acts of service and my heart is more apt to get with the program!

I think an overemphasis on sin, repentance, and salvation (constantly focusing on whether we or others are in or out of God's Kingdom) can deter us from a more effective approach to walking with God.

Instead, we can grab the freedom Jesus paid for on the cross and use it – instead of our obedience merit badge – as permission to serve and grow.

GROW THROUGH PRAYER

Ever share a problem that's been eating at you, only to have your friend ask, "have you prayed about it?"

That can be a frustrating response.

The topic of prayer changing hearts takes me back to going through my conversation with Manny. Remember how my Christmases changed?

The conversation Manny and I had was over a list: steps four and five in our twelve-step process. The main feature was a list of resentments. Mine happened to be extremely long. The list had four columns: who I was upset with, what they did, how it affected me, and my role in it. My problem was I couldn't see my role in any of them, so for hours on end I argued with Manny. I was arguing with a cigarette smoking, 5'5" Bostonian Hulk Hogan lookalike, and things were getting heated!

When we got to the part of the list about my dad, Manny

stopped asking about my role. This was good because I had a full page to read, each line a different gripe.

My dad is a good dad. I'm a good son. That doesn't mean we see eye-to-eye on anything. In fact, I remember conflict going back to age four or so. The result is a pretty long list of resentments.

Nothing on my list referred to any kind of abuse; at its worst, our conflict involved a somewhat stubborn middle-aged dad trying to get an insecure egomaniac kid to comply with his wishes.

I continued reading down the list. After one resentment, Manny got excited, started forward in his chair, and asked, "That one, Andy! What was your role in that one?"

"Manny, I was four! I don't think I had a role in that!"

Manny replied, "You're right. You didn't have a role in it."

Manny's voice softened as he looked me in the eyes. "Your parents loved you and they did the best they could. You need to pray for the willingness to forgive your dad."

At the time, I had no desire to forgive my dad for whatever it was I had read. After all, I was right, he was wrong. I wanted vindication and justice, not a lecture about forgiveness!

But I didn't want to drink again. The offer to me was I either adopt a practice of spiritual growth or drinking would be my fate. So, I prayed for something I didn't want: the willingness to forgive my dad.

A few months went by, and something changed in me. When I thought about my dad, I didn't think about the conflicts we had. I thought about the personal sacrifices he made for our family. How he avoided new cars, fancy clothes, and expensive vacations so he could afford to pay for our educations. All the dad-stuff you'd hope to get, my siblings and I got. My dad remained faithful and a good husband to my mom. They had been together 64 years when she died. How could I ask for more in a father?

A few months after this change of heart, my dad and I went on a bike ride across Iowa called "RAGBRAI." It was a week-long trip, averaging a little over 60 miles each day through corn fields and river valleys.

The long, tiring rides, hot summer sun, and unrelenting humidity made it a challenge. There were additional hardships like flat tires, rainstorms, and the ease with which we could lose each other among the 15,000 daily riders. We slept in tents every night and got up early to avoid some of the afternoon heat. It was no surprise the motto of the event was, "If you're not having fun, you need to lower your standards."

It was the perfect environment for father-son angst.

Despite the deck being stacked against us, we got along great. I never would have imagined appreciating my dad so much, and what a blessing that could be in my life.

What prayers get answered? I can tell you from the Bible and from my experience: prayers that avail myself to know and share God's love in a non-self-aggrandizing way. Those prayers get answered.

PRAYING FOR GOD'S WILL

Thinking about what Jesus taught us in prayer, I'm often reminded of his struggle in the Garden of Gethsemane. He prayed,

"My Father, if it is not possible for this cup to be taken away unless I drink it, may your will be done." (Matt. 26:42)

Jesus was in his mid-thirties. He knew His time had come;

after being betrayed, he was to be arrested, tortured, and put to death.

Jesus didn't even pray for His death on the cross not to happen. Instead, He prayed for the Father's will. The result was the most significant event in human history.

Today, I pray with that in mind. God may have work for me to do that doesn't require curing my sexuality. He may have work for me to do that comes before my overblown ego deflates a little. He may decide to use me in powerful ways, regardless of how much or little I sin. God gets to make those decisions.

If I'm praying for God's will, I'll always get what I pray for. If I pray for what I want instead, I'll still get what God ordained in the first place. The difference is how I receive it; how happy I get to be in God's world, versus how frustrated I can be in Andy's world.

When I pray, I pray for God to allow me to see how events connect to His will. I pray for Him to remove obstacles in the way of my doing His will. I ask for clarity in purpose so I can enjoy walking hand in hand with Him. When I'm particularly upset, I ask for the willingness to accept God's will for my life and for those around me.

GROW IN CHURCH

I met Matt on Facebook after a friend sent out a post about a book study he was hosting. Over the next several weeks, Matt ran a Zoom discussion group for gay men centered around *The Velvet Rage*, a book about how gay men accept and grow into their sexuality.[1] Matt had a great story to tell about how joining a church changed his life.

Matt grew up in an evangelical, fundamentalist church and

family. The only thing he complained about was the church's focus on shame as the way we approach God. Otherwise, he was active at his church and went to Christian schools. He learned there that being gay was wrong.

Matt realized he was a gay later than some, at the age of 22. He described it as "being caught between two unsafe worlds" of his Christian faith and his sexuality. This put Matt into a tailspin and led to what he described as a nervous breakdown in college, a suicide attempt, and an earnest attempt at conversion therapy which had no effect.

What happened next? Matt had to rethink his relationship with God.

> I was sitting at my kitchen table and I just was a mess. I was depressed. I remember saying to God, 'I'm spending all of my energy, trying not to be gay. And I have so many good gifts that I would love to give the world and I have no energy for any of them. I'm going to make the decision, God, to believe that You love me and accept me and created me this way and just let the chips fall where they may.'
>
> It felt like a 200-pound weight had fallen off my shoulders. And it never came back. I started to walk that road and it became a journey of faith I never expected. My relationship with God deepened in a way that I had never experienced.
>
> To leave that shame behind and welcome in God, who has open arms twenty-four-seven, wrecked my world in the best way possible. I took a wrecking ball to so many of the beliefs and struggles and challenges and theologies that I held for so long. I sat there in the rubble looking up at the stars going, 'wow, I don't have to rebuild that. I don't need that. I can just walk with God.'

Going back to church after that was hard for Matt. When he finally did, he experienced what so many do: the joy of community and grace through service.

> It had been a good 15 years since I last darkened the doors of a church. I flirted with a church here in town for a while. I went three or four times. Church was tough for me after all the rejection, feeling judged, and hearing pastors talk about homosexuality from the stage or pulpit as well as other issues I didn't agree with.
>
> A longtime friend introduced me to the pastors of my current church. Their mission statement was something like, 'we believe that Christianity is about loving people, period.'

Matt helped produce videos for his new church. He also led a book club for gay men, which is how I got to know him. It was during the Covid pandemic's shelter-in-place, and he quickly had 40 guys clamoring to read and talk online just from word-of-mouth promotion. At the end of five weekly meetings, no one wanted it to end. As a result, Matt started a private Facebook group and organized monthly online meetings, which doubled the group's original size the day he created it.

I asked Matt what serving and being a part of an accepting church meant to him:

> Learning how to extend grace and empathy and compassion and mercy to myself over and over and over and over and over again unlocked something in me to be able to do that with other people. It's been a journey of helping other people discover their own ability to nurture that relationship [with God] in whatever way that looks for them.

God works in our lives so that we can then meet the needs that other people have.

I feel like I'm finally a member of a community again, and that feels amazing. I'm starting to welcome some of the trials that come into my life because I've seen the pattern – if I'll relinquish my need to control this, God will take it and turn it into something beautiful.

Going to church may seem a normal recommendation for Christian growth. The challenge is that most of us just go – nothing more. We sit, stand, kneel, raise our hands at the right times, listen to a sometimes-too-long sermon, drop an envelope into the basket as it passes by, and we're on our way home!

Matt's story illustrates the difference between simply attending church and doing church. His spiritual life is better for it, and so could be yours!

ANSWERING GOD'S CALL

If you find a place to serve and grow, and pay attention to your progress, you'll see the contribution you make to your community grow. You'll have the opportunity to see how God works through something as simple as your availability. It can feel natural because God has this way of allowing you to be yourself to be of maximum service.

Don't believe me? Look at Jesus' disciples!

Jesus called Matthew, a veritable party animal, to ministry by inviting him to a party (Luke 5:27-29). He called Simon Peter and his brother Andrew, two fishermen, with an offer to go fishing (Matt 4:19). Reading Luke, one can tell it was written by a doctor – because that's what Luke was.

God didn't deny their identities, He affirmed them – even celebrated them! The one common factor in all of these stories was God used who they were as individuals to help others.

With this in mind, your calling may not be difficult to move toward. God is simply calling you to be the most authentic "you." It's exciting to think that what God has available for you to do uses the stuff that makes you "you."

GROW IN VALUE

What do you think of self-esteem?

It's a tough concept to fall in love with – especially after the past few decades have attached requirements for self-esteem like "everyone gets a trophy." Add to that a Christian ethic that seems to sacrifice self-love in favor of "deny yourself, pick up your cross, and follow Jesus," and the idea goes over like, well, a fart in church!

Defining the word "esteem" might help us approach it a bit differently: Esteem simply means value or worth.

With that in mind, what do you think of self-esteem? Is it important for us to be aware of our self-value?

Thinking of self-worth, I'm taken back to my karate days, which were intense, but brief, due to my lack of interest in being kicked.

"Hit him, Andy! As hard as you want!"

I was twenty-one, at college. The karate instructor encouraged me to punch the seventeen-year-old blue belt in the gut – and I hesitated. This seemed a bit weird to just hit someone! The teen grinned and squared his stance.

"Don't worry, he can take a punch."

So, I hit him as hard as I could. It looked like he didn't even feel it.

The kid had a high capacity for impact, it was real, and he knew it. Or to put it another way, he knew the value of his stomach muscles, and knew how much of a punch he could take; to him I didn't look like much of a threat.

When I think about self-value, I think of that punch – or more accurately, the instructor's admonition: "he can take a punch."

Someone who knows their worth can take a punch.

Someone who knows their worth doesn't need a trophy.

They can be called names and respond with love.

They don't need the credit from the boss – they know their work doesn't need to be seen to be valuable.

They're okay living with the disapproval of others when they know they've done nothing wrong.

In other words, they can take a punch!

On the other hand, a person of low self-esteem must have the reward, recognition, and acclaim. They can't handle being called a name. They must win, no matter the expense to others. In fact, winning at the expense of others seems to come naturally to them.

People of low self-esteem cannot afford the grace to allow

another to have what they themselves are terrified to give. They are in an economy of starvation, and to survive, they must hoard the things listed above to feel as though they're of any value.

That's when ego kicks in. Reading the above, you may have recognized the description of high self-esteem is akin to a humble person, and low self-esteem describes an egomaniac. I know this well; left to my own devices, I am an egomaniac!

Of the two described above, who would you rather hang out with? Which would you rather be?

Knowing this about self-esteem, would you be willing to build yours? I'm not saying you have a problem, but on the spectrum of egocentric to fully humble, would you benefit from some work to build your self-esteem as part of your growth toward humility?

BUILDING SELF-ESTEEM

Manny was upset with me one day. It seemed my ego was running my life and he noticed, so he decided it was time to set me straight (so to speak).

"Andy, get out there and do some nice things for people – only I don't want them to know it was you. Do it in secret. You can't tell anyone what you do – not even me. Understand?"

"Where's the fun in that?" I thought to myself. After all, the reward in doing nice things for people was the thanks I got – but again, the threat of drinking drove me to figure out what this new assignment would look like.

Once again, my Jewish sponsor was giving me sage Christian advice. After all, Jesus said,

Be careful not to practice your righteousness in front of others to be seen by them. If you do, you will have no reward from your Father in heaven...But when you give to the needy, do not let your left hand know what your right hand is doing, so that your giving may be in secret. Then your Father, who sees what is done in secret, will reward you. (Matt. 6:1-4)

I knew this already, but the application was different. I used to think of my good works and God's rewards being treasures I stored up in heaven. It was kind of a spiritual bank account for a heavenly retirement plan.

I set out to complete the mission Manny sent me on and serve people in secret.

All of a sudden, I had a role to play that was solely between God and me. It was a great experience, and I have no idea how I've gone more than a decade without divulging the details to anyone. The anonymity I thought would ruin the fun is what made it a rich spiritual experience with God.

With this assignment, the rewards were here and now. I experienced my self-worth. I was working — and walking — hand in hand with God.

The key to building self-esteem, simply put, is to esteem others.

The way I see God's activity today is that there is one essential partner in the results, and that's God. I have the privilege to tag along and help, which is rewarding if I do it properly.

Walking hand in hand with God? The thought that once perplexed me now inspires me.

TO PARENTS, FAMILY AND FRIENDS

When I spoke with John Smid, former director at the ex-gay ministry Love in Action, he recommended writing a chapter to parents and loved ones of LGBTQ people, as they have a lot to deal with. When a friend or loved one comes out, they've had a long time to think about it. Not so for the person on the receiving end.

Christian parents can have an especially tough time dealing with their kids coming out to them. Parents and other close relations, including friends, family, partners, and loved ones can take note of the intense power their reaction can have in the mind and in the life of a person who shares their sexuality with them.

PLACING A BET: PASCAL'S WAGER AND COMING OUT

I read an email from a father to his son about being gay. The father implored him to choose a life of celibacy and faith over being gay, as he was sure that would be a life of sin and separation from God:

What I am begging you to understand is this: the most you will risk with the path I'm calling you to is that you will have unnecessarily forfeited romantic, marital love for a few decades here, a love that is not always fulfilling anyway. And like I said, you won't have lost anything here for Christ's sake that God will not repay you for multifold in the life to come. With this path, you have Heaven at the end either way. The other road is eternally too great a risk.[1]

The father's reasoning is an application of an idea called "Pascal's Wager," named after its creator, Blaise Pascal.

Blaise Pascal was a French mathematician and theologian in the 1600s. Among his many contributions, Pascal came up with the idea that if you're choosing between belief in God and a holy life, versus an atheistic life, you're better off choosing the holy life. He came to this conclusion based on the consequences for being wrong – if you choose a life of non-belief and God does in fact exist, you're in big trouble. If you choose a life of belief in God and you're wrong, there's no ill consequence (except all the fun you missed out on as a sinner).

So, according to Pascal, it's better to believe in God.

PASCAL'S WAGER IS ABOUT BELIEF IN GOD, NOT SEXUAL ORIENTATION

Pascal's Wager is about faith. The dad quoted earlier threatening his son with eternal damnation was betting on behavior rather than belief as the way we seal the deal with God and Heaven. The wager he made assumed God required our obedience to certain rules in addition to our faith in Jesus to be saved. But Pascal's Wager is about faith, not behavior.

You may think it's your kid who's making the wager. I believe instead that you are the one making a wager when responding to them coming out with statements like, "We love you, but we don't agree with this," or, "We love you, but you know this is a sin, right?" or, "We love you, even though you're…"

The wager is placed on what will happen when a parent alienates their kids for the sake of their faith.

THE REAL WAGER

As the parent or friend of someone who comes out, you are the one with a bet to make. You can affirm them as they have presented themselves to you, or not affirm them with as much love as you can muster so they get the right idea of what God's economy of righteous behavior is all about.

If you aren't supportive, you're betting that the pain of your admonishment will be enough to drive them to a better decision about their life. You're betting they'll find a way to live in light of that decision. Perhaps conversion therapy or celibacy will work for them?

If you choose not to affirm their sexuality, you're betting that your child has a choice; that they can find an alternative that will work for them. Of course, there's a possibility your gay child or friend doesn't have a choice about their orientation. Traditional options may not work for them.

Perhaps you're betting that your child is wrong. While they think they're gay (or trans, or bi, or lesbian, or asexual, etc.), you may be betting it's just a phase. If it's not a phase, you're betting they can overcome this, with God's help, through conversion or celibacy.

What happens if they fail? You're betting they won't. Because if they fail, the message is clear: God's not into gay kids. They'll be out of the "I'm going to heaven" club. That's a heck of a thing to live with!

None of these bets are made by the person who's just come out to you. They're yours to make. Perhaps before you place your first bet, you should have a look at the odds?

HOW THE DECK IS STACKED

If you're betting that opposing your kid's sexuality will have a positive impact on their lives and eternal souls, let me point out some facts and figures.

First, when teenagers come out at home and aren't accepted, they have a significantly higher rate of homelessness. This isn't because their parents kick them out. It's because the tension of living in an unaccepting household drives them out eventually.[2]

LGBTQ youth are eight times more likely to attempt suicide when in non-accepting homes.[3,4]

LGBTQ youth have higher suicide attempt rates if they attend conversion therapy.[5]

Elsewhere in this book we looked at the abysmal failure rates found in celibacy and conversion therapy attempts. Why would anyone place this bet given these odds?

If the well-being of the person who comes out to us is our concern, the best results lie in support, not criticism. The most loving thing is to be a place of safety. But just how do we do that?

BRING ON THE MAMA BEARS

Liz Dyer runs a private Facebook group comprised of more than 22,000 mothers of LGBTQ children called "Mama Bears." You can find them at www.realmamabears.org, along with support groups for friends and family of those moms, and a story site for moms who want to share with others their experiences handling their kids coming out to them. She's several years into this service and knows a couple of things about the needs of LGBTQ kids and their parents!

Liz's son came out to her when he was 19. He had known he was gay since he was 12 but didn't come out because he was afraid of what his parents' reaction would be.

Liz told me:

> It was a bumpy road for us. I never disowned my son. I never said he was going to go to hell, but I certainly thought it was wrong. I thought he needed to either try to do something to change or be celibate.[6]

Liz was an active conservative Christian; she led women's groups at her church and attended several functions a week there in addition to Sunday services. Her church wasn't supportive of gays, and neither was she.

When her son came out, Liz did some homework and learned as much as she could about homosexuality in the Bible and alternatives for LGBTQ people of faith:

> My husband and I went on a sincere journey of discovery. And honestly it did not take me long at all to realize that Scripture

actually did not answer my questions. It did not talk about the kind of relationship that my son was talking about having.

There was nothing in Scripture about anybody dating someone of the same sex, falling in love, getting married, or having a family. The few passages that were about same-sex relationships were about pagan rituals or powerful men taking young boys as prostitutes. There was one verse that maybe could be applied, but it didn't fit because it talked about people turning away from God and lusting for other things.

My son wasn't doing that. My son was pretty conservative and traditional. He loved God. He loved the church. He wanted to do the right things.

When he talked to me about it, he would say, 'you know, it's not like I want to have some wild, sex same-sex relationship. I want to have a same-sex relationship in the same context that my brother wants to have a heterosexual relationship; that you and dad wanted to have a relationship. I want to have a real, loving, committed relationship, but with someone of the same sex.'

So, those verses didn't fit my point. And still, when you have been on this journey your whole life thinking something is wrong, you don't change your mind at the snap of a finger. I thought, if I can't get the answer from Scripture, I'm going to have to get the answer somewhere else.

We can always find a Bible verse, a book, a community, a pastor, a group of people, a friend, a family member who will agree with us, no matter what side we take on this issue. We can all prop up our position by these things. But we cannot manipulate the fruit that is produced by the ideas and values and ways of living that people embrace. When people embrace non-affirming LGBTQ theology, it almost always produces negative fruit. It almost always produces depression, anxiety, isolation, self-loathing even suicidal ideation to some degree in most people. But when LGBTQ people accept that they're LGBTQ and start to embrace affirming LGBTQ theology, affirming ideas, affirming perspectives, and connect with others that embrace those ideas, they are typically more healthy, more whole in every way.

I say the fruit doesn't lie. The fruit reveals truth to us. Jesus said a bad tree cannot produce good fruit and a good tree cannot produce bad fruit.

These things that I knew about Scripture and looking at real life situations are the things that gave me complete peace of mind to become 100% affirming.

As for advice to Christian parents whose kids come out, Liz narrows it down to a few key pointers, starting with, "don't drag your feet!"

In fact, when Liz came out of her "closet" as the mother of a gay young man, she left her volunteer position in the church. That bothered her – but what bothered her more was she hadn't done it sooner.

Liz points out,

I want to support parents, but I also want to challenge them. Don't drag your feet!

There's a saying that when Christian kids come out of the closet, their Christian parents go in the closet. That happens a lot. Not because they don't love their kids, but there's a lot of fear. And there's a lot to lose.

I wasn't there for my son. I felt robbed. I felt cheated. I felt betrayed by the church. I can never go back and change that.

When we know better, we can do better. My son has completely forgiven me. We have a wonderful relationship, but it still breaks my heart to know that he was going through that alone.

ADVICE FROM 22,000 MOMS

Here's Liz's advice, after virtually meeting 22,000 moms who have gone through this process along with her, in four key steps:

Let them know you love them unconditionally

You have to let your child know immediately that you love them unconditionally that no matter what their sexual orientation is, no matter what their gender identity is, you love them unconditionally for who they are for the person they are.

Nothing's ever going to change that. You're not going to reject them. You're not going to walk away from them. You love them and you're going to figure this out together. I think that is the most important thing. We must let our kids know; that is the utmost thing.

Our kids come to us afraid of what our reaction will be. They've been processing this for a long time, and we need to immediately do what we can to relieve some of that anxiety and give them reassurance.

Find support

You're going to have a lot of fears. You're going to have doubts. You're going to have questions, and that is normal. You need to find support. I'm not going to ever suggest that you should suppress or deny anything that you're feeling; that's not a healthy way to deal with it. Just keep it away from your kid!

Don't look to your kid for support. Don't look to your kid to answer a lot of your questions.

You can ask your kid to share their story with you and show interest: What's it been like for you? What are your biggest fears? Have you told others? How do you want to handle this going forward?

Liz recommends finding other parents who have worked through this to learn from and lean on. Her groups and website are a great place to start.

Educate yourself

Liz recommends using Google, PFLAG (Parents, Families and Friends of Lesbians and Gays), and other resources to learn as much as you can about LGBTQ people and their issues to combat the fear of the unknown, as she's noticed in the parents she's worked with over the years,

The number one emotion that mothers have is fear of the unknown. What is this going to mean for their child? What's this going to mean for their day-to-day life, for their career, for their relationships, for their safety? These are the things that mothers are most concerned about, and this fear can be paralyzing.

Paralyzing, as in keeping parents from being there for their kids when they're needed most.

Let them know you'll do everything to let them confidently be their best selves

Liz believes a parent's opportunity is to allow their kids to become the best version of the person they were created to be.

Four critical elements will help you with your LGBTQ child

or friend: Communicate your unconditional love, find support, get educated, and let them know you're there for them as they grow!

WHAT'S MY JOB?

The key when approaching the topic of "what do I do when someone I care about comes out" is to realize that God does not ask for our help convicting, chastising, or judging His children; He's provided for that already with His Holy Spirit. What God has given us is the charge to love one another as He loves us.

While it may seem easy to diagnose and correct sin, most people I know find it more challenging to accept others for who they are – just as they are. That's how Jesus accepts you and me, so we have a pretty clear example of our task. The next steps involve working out our love through acceptance, gathering support, doing some research, and instilling confidence in our loved ones that we'll be there for them, no matter what!

WE'RE PREGNANT!

"I've got some news for all of you: You're all pregnant!"

Ken Medema smiled as he looked around the auditorium at the packed church in Pasadena. Some of us chuckled, unsure of what to make of his announcement – we were there for a Christmas concert, not a visit to the doctor.

Ken Medema is a musician and a music therapist. For decades he has entertained and healed with his unique gift of song. Blind from birth, there's no reading set lists, notes, or sheet music. The special bonus is, Ken can write a song in his head about your story as you tell it to him and play it moments later with every detail carefully remembered and sung while playing along on his piano.

Well into his fifties, Ken's mannerisms, tenor voice, and wispy white hair reminded me of Doc from the movie *Back to the Future*. The way he moved his head and body around the piano and keyboards, wildly singing high notes with tremendous passion and volume, only to reduce to a whisper for an important lyric made him come off as a little crazy to me – but genius, whimsical crazy.

"You're all pregnant!" Ken repeated. "God wants to give birth to something WONDERFUL through YOU!"

It was his introduction to a song about what Mary must have felt like learning she was pregnant. Ken went on to explain that we all come bearing God's gifts for our world. It was our job to deliver them. I never forgot the way that made me feel.

When I think of Ken's proposal, that we've all got something growing inside us that will bless the world, I think of the people I met writing this book.

Stan Mitchell counsels LGBTQ Christians, their parents, and churches every day on what it means to follow Jesus in light of their sexuality. Out of losing much of the life he built, he's giving birth to something wonderful!

Alice faithfully served a church and reconciled her relationship with her parents. She found a church to serve meaningfully and a wonderful career. Now retired, she stays active in church and in her faith.

Paul Fromberg pastors a church that innovates worship and ministry in a unique way. Paul continues to be a gift to our congregation. He uses his gifts as a teacher, a pastor, an artist, and a writer to reach a lot of people. You may enjoy his books *The Art of Disruption: Improvisation and the Book of Common Prayer* and *The Art of Transformation: Three Things Churches Do That Change Everything.*[1]

I'm grateful that Reverend Jeff Harris answered his call to ministry instead of burying his head in the "I'm gay so I can't be a pastor" sand. In an hour on the phone, he taught me a few things about the Gospel – especially that the point of this life isn't limited to ensuring our role in the next one. His message is that we need to answer our call in this world.

Matt's monthly online meeting has grown to where he now

has guest speakers and an increasing number of breakout rooms for large and small group discussions. A lot of us are ironing out our faith and the group is a great place to share that journey!

Ann, Darrell's mom, who inspired me to write this book, continues to be a fierce ally for her kids. Ann's home has become a shelter for kids who are dealing with their sexuality and need to take some heat off (with their parents' permission). She takes the Mama Bear role and organization very seriously and can be seen at various community events with a Free Mom Hugs tee shirt (another ally organization).[2]

Big and small, these people are making impacts on this world, and the impacts have love written all over them. The obvious next question is, what's your contribution going to be?

BRING IT!

As LGBTQ Christians, we have something unique to bring to the world. Everything we've gone through and will go through, combined with who we are as individuals, help shape that gift. The exciting thing about our gifts is they're a bit of a mystery.

Think about handing someone a Christmas present, uniquely from you, but being just as excited to see what it is as they are! That's what our lives can be when we serve the God of Love through Jesus.

The things that stand in the way of letting this gift come out can be easily removed – it only takes a little willingness and a bit of faith. It starts with knowing that we can take a chance with our service because of security in God's love.

Even if you're still having trouble with the arguments about homosexuality in the Bible, you have permission – not from me, but from the Gospel - to accept God's grace instead of fighting an unwinnable battle that drags so many to despair. That's how you can cast off the sin that keeps you from delivering God's gift that you can uniquely bestow on our world.

The best part of all this is you don't have to do it alone. There are congregations genuinely excited to have you with them. They will be there for you as you are there for them.

Jesus said,

Come to me, all you who are weary and burdened, and I will give you rest. Take my yoke upon you and learn from me, for I am gentle and humble in heart, and you will find rest for your souls. For my yoke is easy and my burden is light. (Matt. 11:28-30)

I pray that you and those you love find Jesus' promise true in your lives.

God loves you and has a wonderful plan for your life!

NOTES

Preface

1. Colby Martin, *UnClobber: Rethinking Our Misuse of the Bible on Homosexuality* (Westminster John Knox Press, 2016).

Trying to be Straight

1. "The Four Spiritual Laws - In Your Language!," accessed March 19, 2021, http://www.4laws.com/laws/languages.html.
2. J.P. Moreland, "JP Moreland's Web» The 'Nashville Statement,'" Blog, J.P. Moreland, September 8, 2017, http://www.jpmoreland.com/2017/09/08/the-nashville-statement/.

Coming to Terms

1. "There Is No Such Thing as Gay People, Los Angeles Pastor Claims," *Pink-News - Gay News, Reviews and Comment from the World's Most Read Lesbian, Gay, Bisexual, and Trans News Service* (blog), June 29, 2017, https://www.pinknews.co.uk/2017/06/29/there-is-no-such-thing-as-gay-people-los-angeles-pastor-claims/.
2. Dale Carnegie, *How to Win Friends and Influence People*, 32d ed (New York: Simon and Schuster, 1937), pts. 2, Ch.3.
3. "Comedian Carlin Leaves Rich Legacy," NPR.org, accessed October 9, 2020, https://www.npr.org/templates/story/story.php?storyId=91819121.
4. Richard A Cohen, *Coming out Straight: Understanding and Healing Homosexuality* (Winchester, Va.: Oakhill Press, 2000), http://books.google.com/books?id=0zEQAQAAMAAJ.
5. Many have discovered through their own stories they didn't have an "alternative," so it's not appropriate to use this label.

A Faith that Works: Can God Cure Me?

1. Katherine S. Milar, "The Myth Buster," *Monitor on Psychology* 42, no. 2 (February 2011): 24.

2. Conger, J.J. (1975). Proceedings of the American Psychological Association, Incorporated, for the year 1974: Minutes of the annual meeting of the Council of Representatives. American Psychologist, 30, 620-651. (accessed at https://www.apa.org/about/policy/discrimination)

3. Kent Philpott, *The Third Sex? Six Homosexuals Tell Their Stories* (Plainfield, N.J: Logos International, 1975), 163–64.

4. "Former 'Ex-Gay' Leader: These Programs Are Harmful and Don't Work," January 16, 2019, https://www.advocate.com/commentary/2019/1/16/former-ex-gay-leader-these-programs-are-harmful-and-dont-work.

5. "What Does the Scholarly Research Say about Whether Conversion Therapy Can Alter Sexual Orientation without Causing Harm?," What We Know, accessed May 20, 2021, https://whatweknow.inequality.cornell.edu/topics/lgbt-equality/what-does-the-scholarly-research-say-about-whether-conversion-therapy-can-alter-sexual-orientation-without-causing-harm/.

6. Tanya Erzen, *Straight to Jesus: Sexual and Christian Conversions in the Ex-Gay Movement* (Berkeley: University of California Press, 2006), 34.

7. Erzen, 63.

8. Chris Bull, "Finding a Real Cure," *The Advocate*, September 26, 2000.

9. Wayne R. Besen, *Anything but Straight: Unmasking the Scandals and Lies behind the Ex-Gay Myth* (New York: Harrington Park Press, 2003), 4, 16.

10. Zoë Schlanger and Elijah Wolfson On 5/1/14 at 11:36 AM EDT, "Ex-Ex-Gay Pride," Newsweek, May 1, 2014, https://www.newsweek.com/ex-ex-gay-pride-249282; Truth Wins Out, *Truth In Love Campaign: Failed Michael Jonston Ad Backfires*, 2013, https://www.youtube.com/watch?v=BatBfWZJo78.

11. Besen, *Anything but Straight*, 119–21, 223.

12. "John Smid, Former 'Ex-Gay' Leader, Marries A Man In Oklahoma | HuffPost," accessed March 21, 2021, https://www.huffpost.com/entry/john-smid-ex-gay-wedding-_n_6186524.

13. "Former 'Ex-Gay' Leader."

14. Penn Bullock Thorp Brandon K., "Christian Right Leader George Rekers Takes Vacation with 'Rent Boy,'" Miami New Times, May 6, 2010, https://www.miaminewtimes.com/news/christian-right-leader-george-rekers-takes-vacation-with-rent-boy-6377933.

15. "Gay Men Sue Counselors Who Promised to Make Them Straight | CNN," accessed May 20, 2021, https://www.cnn.com/2012/11/27/us/conversion-therapy-lawsuit/index.html.

16. Benedict Carey, "Psychiatry Giant Sorry for Backing Gay 'Cure,'" *The New York Times*, May 18, 2012, sec. Health, https://www.nytimes.com/2012/05/19/health/dr-robert-l-spitzer-noted-psychiatrist-apologizes-for-study-on-gay-cure.html.

17. Ian Lovett, "After 37 Years of Trying to Change People's Sexual Orientation, Group Is to Disband," *The New York Times*, June 20, 2013, sec. U.S., 37, https://www.nytimes.com/2013/06/21/us/group-that-promoted-curing-gays-ceases-operations.html.

18. Erik Eckholm, "Rift Forms in Movement as Belief in Gay 'Cure' Is Renounced," *The New York Times*, July 7, 2012, sec. U.S., https://www.nytimes.com/2012/07/07/us/a-leaders-renunciation-of-ex-gay-tenets-causes-a-schism.html.

19. Michael Majchrowicz mmajchrowicz@postandcourier.com, "Conversion Therapy Leader for 2 Decades, McKrae Game Disavows Movement He Helped Fuel," Post and Courier, accessed May 20, 2021, https://www.postandcourier.com/news/conversion-therapy-leader-for-2-decades-mckrae-game-disavows-movement-he-helped-fuel/article_fb56dcfc-c384-11e9-970d-bb9a2a8656c5.html.

20. Julie Compton, "Once-Prominent 'Conversion Therapist' Will Now 'Pursue Life as a Gay Man,'" NBC News, accessed May 20, 2021, https://www.nbcnews.com/feature/nbc-out/once-prominent-conversion-therapist-will-now-pursue-life-gay-man-n961766.

21. "Former Gay Conversion Therapy Leader Comes Out, Apologizes to LGBTQ Community," Time, accessed May 20, 2021, https://time.com/5668351/mckrae-game-comes-out-gay-conversion/.

22. "Former Ex-Lesbian Leader, Yvette Cantu Schneider, Gives the Inside Scoop on Conversion Programs in New TWO Pride Month Interview Series | Truth Wins Out," accessed May 20, 2021, https://truthwinsout.org/pressrelease/2019/06/41826/.

23. "Former 'Ex-Gay' Leader."

24. Melissa Steffan, "Former Ex-Gay Spokesman John Paulk Apologizes Amid Divorce," News & Reporting, accessed May 20, 2021, https://www.christianitytoday.com/news/2013/may/former-ex-gay-spokesman-john-paulk-apologizes-amid-divorce.html.

25. "Former Gay Conversion Therapy Leader Comes Out, Apologizes to LGBTQ Community."

26. Michael Bussee, "Michael Bussee Ex-Gay Leader Apology - Beyond Ex-Gay," accessed May 20, 2021, https://beyondexgay.com/article/busseeapology.html.

27. Melissa Steffan, "Alan Chambers Apologizes to Gay Community, Exodus International to Shut Down," News & Reporting, accessed March 21, 2021,

https://www.christianitytoday.com/news/2013/june/alan-chambers-apolo-gizes-to-gay-community-exodus.html.

Celibacy

1. Christopher Yuan and Rosaria Butterfield, *Holy Sexuality and the Gospel: Sex, Desire, and Relationships Shaped by God's Grand Story* (Colorado Springs: Mult-nomah, 2018).
2. Yuan and Butterfield, 63.
3. *Spiritual Friendship by Wesley Hill - Book - Read Online*, accessed April 1, 2020, https://www.scribd.com/book/259698972/Spiritual-Friendship-Finding-Love-in-the-Church-as-a-Celibate-Gay-Christian.
4. *Spiritual Friendship by Wesley Hill - Book - Read Online.* p. 43
5. Yuan and Butterfield, *Holy Sexuality and the Gospel*, 123.
6. Yuan and Butterfield, 123.

Putting Things in Perspective

1. "Nashville Statement," CBMW, accessed March 21, 2021, https://cbmw.org/nashville-statement/.
2. "Masturbation: Opposition by Conservative Protestants," accessed May 20, 2021, http://www.religioustolerance.org/masturba6.htm.
3. To clarify, removing the personhood of your sex partner is a scary, dangerous thing in my opinion.
4. "Q&A – A Question About Masturbation," accessed August 10, 2021, https://www.dobsonlibrary.com/resource/article/62636b45-ecd9-4346-afde-aa6681775ce2?fbclid=IwAR2FQF9NucRTtcxMV2nTyANO1TV_-mo29lCDyYOdH-t7OfwkvIhb7tW7grnI.
5. "Teen Struggling With Masturbation - Focus on the Family," accessed March 20, 2021, https://www.focusonthefamily.com/family-qa/teen-struggling-with-masturbation/.

What the Bible Says

1. Mark A. Noll, *When God & Science Meet: Surprising Discoveries of Agreement*, accessed April 18, 2020, https://www.scribd.com/book/267681628/When-God-Science-Meet-Surprising-Discoveries-of-Agreement. p. 16
2. Noll. p. 16

3. *The Civil War as a Theological Crisis*, accessed April 18, 2020, https://www.scribd.com/book/322777925/The-Civil-War-as-a-Theological-Crisis. p. 61-74

4. Earl Radmacher, "How to Know What the Bible Means by What It Says" (Western Conservative Baptist Seminary, 1996).

5. "Pig-Latin" is a fake language kids sometimes use, putting the first letter of each word at the end along with the hard vowel sound for "A." "Bad luck," then, is "adbay ucklay" in pig-Latin.

6. Martin, *UnClobber*, 161.

7. Rabbi Bruce Warshal, "Lots of Abominations in the Bible," *South Florida Sun Sentinal, Florida Jewish Journal*, September 19, 2012, https://www.sun-sentinel.com/florida-jewish-journal/fl-xpm-2012-09-19-fl-jjps-warshal-0919-20120919-story.html.

8. Warshal.

9. Henry Virkler, *Hermeneutics: Principles and Processes of Biblical Interpretation*, 22, accessed April 18, 2020, https://www.scribd.-com/book/340147951/Hermeneutics-Principles-and-Processes-of-Biblical-Interpretation.

10. Martin, *UnClobber*, 136.

11. David Lose, ContributorSenior Pastor, and Mount Olivet Lutheran Church, "What Does The Bible Really Say About Homosexuality?," HuffPost, 56:12 400AD, https://www.huffpost.com/entry/what-does-the-bible-real-l_b_990444.

12. Robert H. Allen, *The Classical Origins of Modern Homophobia* (Jefferson, N.C: McFarland, 2006), 187.

13. Bernard L. Ramm, *Protestant Biblical Interpretation: A Textbook of Hermeneutics*, 3d rev. ed (Grand Rapids: Baker Book House, 1970), 105.

Beware the Bait and Switch Gospel

1. Paul Suggett, "Understand the Bait-And-Switch Scam," *The Balance Careers* (blog), accessed October 9, 2019, https://www.thebalancecareers.com/un-derstand-the-bait-and-switch-scam-38480.

2. *The Holy Bible: King James Version.* (2009). (Electronic Edition of the 1900 Authorized Version., Jn 3:16). Bellingham, WA: Logos Research Systems, Inc.

3. Josh McDowell, *More than a Carpenter* (New York: Walker and Co., 1977).

The Gospel for Gay People

1. Martin, Colby "Unclobber: Rethinking Our Misuse of the Bible on Homosexuality," Westminster John Knox Press: 2016.

2. "The Doctrine of Salvation: Assurance," Grace to You, accessed May 20, 2021, https://www.gty.org/library/sermons-library/DOC-13/.

3. "How Christians Have Misunderstood Grace," accessed May 20, 2021, https://religionnews.com/2014/07/17/christians-misunderstood-grace/.

4. "7 Famous Sinners in Christ's Family Tree," accessed May 20, 2021, https://www.beliefnet.com/faiths/christianity/7-famous-sinners-in-christs-family-tree.aspx.

5. Frank E. Gaebelein and J. D. Douglas, eds., *The Expositor's Bible Commentary: With the New International Version of the Holy Bible*, vol. 12 (Grand Rapids: Zondervan Pub. House, 1976), 134.

Coming Out

1. Mel White, *Stranger at the Gate: To Be Gay and Christian in America* (New York: Simon & Schuster, 1994).

Sex, Relationships, and Marriage

1. Norman L. Geisler and Thomas A. Howe, *When Critics Ask: A Popular Handbook on Bible Difficulties* (Wheaton, Ill.: Victor Books, 1992), 365.

2. "Types of Marriages in the Bible, and Today," accessed September 6, 2020, http://www.religioustolerance.org/mar_bibl0a.htm.

3. Virkler, *Hermeneutics*, 115.

4. Sarah Ruden, *Paul among the People: The Apostle Reinterpreted and Reimagined in His Own Time* (New York: Pantheon Books, 2010), 35–36.

Choosing a Church

1. Earl D. Radmacher, *The Nature of the Church* (Hayesville, NC: Schoettle Pub. Co., 1996), 273.

2. Radmacher, 352.

3. Anthony Venn-Brown, *A Life of Unlearning: Coming out of the Church, One Man's Struggle* (Sydney: New Holland, 2015).

4. Harris, Jeff, Andy Wells Interview with Reverend Jeff Harris, Internet call, September 7, 2020.

5. Harris, Jeff, *Called, Claimed, and Commissioned* (National Capital Region, USA: Faith Work Publishing, LLC, 2020).

6. Stan Mitchell, Andy Wells Interview with Stan Mitchell, September 18, 2020.

How to Grow

1. Alan Downs, *The Velvet Rage: Overcoming the Pain of Growing up Gay in a Straight Man's World* (Cambridge, MA: Da Capo Lifelong, 2005).

To Parents, Family and Friends

1. "Stan Mitchell | Facebook," accessed February 13, 2021, https://www.facebook.com/stan.mitchell.58. Quoted with permission.

2. Theo G M Sandfort, "Experiences and Well-Being of Sexual and Gender Diverse Youth in Foster Care in New York City," n.d., 8.

3. "Facts About Suicide," The Trevor Project, accessed February 13, 2021, https://www.thetrevorproject.org/resources/preventing-suicide/facts-about-suicide/.

4. "Research Brief: Accepting Adults Reduce Suicide Attempts Among LGBTQ Youth," The Trevor Project, June 27, 2019, https://www.thetrevorproject.org/2019/06/27/research-brief-accepting-adults-reduce-suicide-attempts-among-lgbtq-youth/.

5. "The Trevor Project National Survey 2019," accessed February 13, 2021, https://www.thetrevorproject.org/survey-2019/.

6. Dyer, Liz, Liz Dyer, Andy Wells Interview, Zoom, January 29, 2021.

We're Pregnant!

1. Paul Fromberg, *The Art of Disruption: Improvisation and the Book of Common Prayer* (New York, New York: Seabury Books, 2021); Paul Fromberg, *The Art of Transformation: Three Things Churches Do That Change Everything* (New York: Church Publishing, 2017).

2. https://freemomhugs.org/

ABOUT THE AUTHOR

Andy Wells is an experienced lay church leader and accomplished speaker. He holds a Master of Arts in Christian Apologetics from Biola University. Andy's education, coupled with his life experience struggling to reconcile his faith and sexuality, lend credibility to his writing.

Andy's passion for the topics of sexuality and faith come from his struggle with self-acceptance. He knows the frustration of living as a secretly gay man and a publicly born-again Christian. Finding a solution that works without having to abandon one's faith is Andy's desire in helping others facing the same dilemma.

For more information : www.triedtobestraight.com

ACKNOWLEDGMENTS

When I began writing this book, my friend and pastor Paul Fromberg told me this might be a good way to gain clarity and closure on several issues in my life. I thought he was patronizing me at the time, but he couldn't have been more right! Writing this book gave me the opportunity to get to know many amazing people – some for the first time and some more deeply. Most of all, I've been able to grow in my relationship with Jesus through this experience and I'm grateful for that.

For the people who encouraged and inspired me to write this book: Lynn Bailey, Wendy Newman, Taz Richards, Becca Manuel, Dave Pierce, and my friends at the Intersection of Sexuality and Spirituality reading group – which has become more of a family than a book club.

Thank you to the members of St. Gregory of Nyssa Episcopal Church for being as close to the ideal church as I've found to date (and yes, you're still whacky). You've all been so wonderful to encourage, mentor, and pray for me along this journey.

To the people who've helped me by reviewing and editing parts and pieces as I wrote, including Megan Hershenson, Colin

Low, Rick Lucke, Lily Zheng, Scotty Streitfeld, Jon Spangler, Reverend Erin Wyma, and Pastor Stan Mitchell: Thank you for your support in so many ways over the past two years. Your skills at writing honed mine, and your candid input helped me immensely.

To my friend Mike Rosebush, thank you for supporting me with your energetic encouragement. I'll never forget how blessed I felt the day you agreed to write the foreword – one of the highlights of this journey!

To the people from whom I gleaned technical knowledge and history of conversion therapy: McKrae Game, thanks for a socially distanced dinner during Covid! Wayne Besen, Michael Bussee, and John Smid, thanks for spending time to help me understand how praying the gay away developed and operated.

Finally, thanks to Yifan, my friend, companion, and true partner for supporting me in so many ways. I love you!

Made in United States
North Haven, CT
12 April 2024

51245083R00109